Dreaming Inside Out

KIRAYA KESTIN

Dreaming Inside Out

Copyright © 2019 by Kiraya Kestin. All rights reserved.

All rights reserved. No part of this publication may be reproduced or transmitted in any form or by any means, electronic or mechanical, including photocopy, recording, or any information storage and retrieval system, without permission in writing from author/publisher.

Request for permission to reproduce this work may be submitted to creationbykiraya@msn.com

My grateful thanks to my editor, Peggy King Anderson for her encouragement and suggestions, also to my proof reader Galina Milohov.

Published in the United States of America

Library of Congress Copyrights: TXu 2-144-516

Dedicated to self-exploration

Contents

Part 1: 1974

Chapter One 3
Chapter Two 8
Chapter Three 13
Chapter Four 17
Chapter Five 20
Chapter Six 23
Chapter Seven 28
Chapter Eight 30
Chapter Nine 34
Chapter Ten 37
Chapter Eleven 42
Chapter Twelve 46
Chapter Thirteen 50
Chapter Fourteen 54
Chapter Fifteen 59
Chapter Sixteen 65

Chapter Seventeen..69
Chapter Eighteen 76
Chapter Nineteen 81
Chapter Twenty...84

Part 2

Chapter Twenty-One...93
Chapter Twenty-Two...98
Chapter Twenty-Three 103
Chapter Twenty-Four 110
Chapter Twenty-Five 115
Chapter Twenty-Six...118
Chapter Twenty-Seven..124
Chapter Twenty-Eight 131
Chapter Twenty-Nine...142

Part 1

1974

Dreaming Inside Out

Chapter One

When I was 28 years old, I decided to record my dreams, because I didn't know what I believed or how God worked in my life. These dreams are what I discovered.

My closed eyelids quiver. I walk across a smooth surface where mist gathers like dust around my ankles. It obscures my view of what's under foot. I know I'm outside, though this place has a definite interior feel, like the warmth of a low ceiling room, but with all the stretching expansion of the outdoors. I don't know where I am, maybe I'm behind stage in a theater, meandering through foggy drop-curtains, but I don't know where I'm going either. Angel hair clouds fade in and out around me as I move forward. Brightness is everywhere, illuminating from the inside out, and no shadows to comprehend. Most of the setting to my right is lost in a steep wall of fog, but to my left there's a small clearing where I see a quaint thatch roofed cottage.

The door opens and out files a group of people chatting and laughing. They are followed by a tall, dark haired man dressed in a black suit with a long cape thrown across his shoulders. He moves with smooth commanding strides into the center of the troupe. I duck cautiously into the fog to hide myself. He begins to give instructions to the company. I wonder if he's a magician, and whether they are preparing to rehearse their magic show? I have a perfect view from my spot to watch unobserved.

The troupe consists of both men and women dressed exactly alike in short white tunics, belted by a thin red leather strap that goes around their waists and over their right shoulders. Their arms and legs are bare and on their feet are high topped, white tennis shoes with little wing shapes on the ankles that jet out behind.

Their leader steps back and gives a signal to start. Immediately, the members of the group begin to raise their bodies into the air stopping at different assigned heights, then smoothly landing to the ground. Moving amongst the troupe, he continues to give individual instructions on precise control of their elevations and direction of movement, stressing the importance of lightly touching ground with gentle poise.

I'm extremely intrigued by these wonder people! It must feel marvelously free to be able to spring up into the atmosphere and hold your position above ground until you're ready to come down again. I'm inspired and I want to be like them.

Let's see here, I glance down at my own feet placing them parallel and about a foot apart. I bend my knees visualizing in my mind the images of what the troupe did. I give a little jump and to my delight I feel my body moving slowly upward about four feet above where I'd been standing! Then I lower myself like an elevator, recalling every detail of what I had heard him tell his troupe. It works! I use my mind to move and direct my body. What I intend to do, controls my action. In a burst of enthusiasm, I rocket higher into the sky, forgetting myself, except to touch down again with deliberate softness. The thrill of success invigorates me. I experiment air born, going sideways, using helicopter accuracy, intent on discovering all I can do.

Then a strange sensation grips my stomach. I raise my eyes from the spot where I just landed and lock eyes with the troupe leader. I'm held by the power of his focused stare. He searches me with quiet kindness, assessing my strength. I've been discovered.

"I see I have a new student. Come and join our troupe."

I nod reluctantly, maybe I'm not good enough, but I'm inspired by what I might learn. I hurry over to the group, not wanting to delay them. The leader sweeps us with his smile. With the gesture of his arms, he gives us another task of moving backwards which I perform correctly. He tests me specifically a couple more times. I seem to be able to do these requests easily. Then he turns and points to a place where the mist parts, about thirty feet away.

"Our next exercise is to jump over the edge." He looks at me. "Can you do that?"

I nod again, inflated by my recent successes, *that won't be difficult at all.* I take a few steps backward and run with gathering speed. Leaping wide, I sail over the drop-off, glancing down as I soar, to see where I'll land. To my instant shock and horror, I discover I have jumped into a sky-blue elevator shaft filled with tiny sparkling stars, and no bottom I can see! Fear, like a bolt of electricity rips through me. I jerk to a stop in mid-air. My only thought is to escape! I plaster myself against the rock cliff just inside the shaft. My fingers and toes grip tiny edges in the surface. Instantly, I change forms. A muscular, black man materializes in my place clinging to the same narrow ledge inside the shaft. He's engulfed in my fear. His knuckles are white with the strain of grasping as his fingers grapple for a better hold. His body is flattened tight against the side of the cliff wall hanging on for his life.

So where am I? I've become a small ball of invisible consciousness floating about five feet above the edge. What I thought was a shaft, turns out to be miles and miles of open space. I'm surprised at how fast I evaded my fear with a substitute. I feel safe and detached, as I observe the scene from my secure spot. It's his problem now.

Then from my peaceful lull, I'm disturbed by a firm voice. "Mary, Mary, let go. Let go and fall to me."

That's my name! I look over to see what's happening. The teacher is standing in the air across from the terrified man. His arms are outstretched to catch him if he tumbles. The teacher continues to call me with infinite patience and total confidence. He's not fooled by my disguise. He knows I can't go forward until I deal with my fear and release this man.

"Just let go and fall. You can do it!"

His voice penetrates the center of me. I don't want to disobey. He didn't abandon me. He wants to help me, and he won't leave without me. I can trust him!

In compassion, I propel myself toward my strong substitute entering into my own fear form and loosening the stiff aching fingers. Feeling my humanness again, I fall in slow motion, backward toward my teacher and into my womanly form. My fear dissolves with the man and is forgotten.

As I'm falling, I twist around and right myself. Warm air ruffles my clothing and my hair streams out above me. Stars dart by me like silver minnows in an ocean of blue space. Contented is how I feel and trusting in the whole of the Universe. Falling, falling through miles of time, no rush, I just look around waiting until I come down.

After a while, I see below me the glow of an open room. I land on tip-toe onto a golden marble floor. My teacher is waiting for me. He nods and spreads out his arm to lead the way. This room reminds me of the center of a huge power source. I can hear a low hum. We arrive at a long platform with three steps up. I see some of the others from our troupe waiting in what looks like glass capsules around the lower part of their bodies. The teacher helps me into this transparent force field and snaps a metal piece around my waist to stabilize me. He signals to us, and steps back. With a shake of his head, yellow shafts of light pour down on us. Revitalizing energy flows into me. I seem to soar and become one with its flow of strength.

I opened my eyes. I sat up in my bed and grabbed my notebook, not wanting to forget that amazing experience, where I saw my fear and felt my glory. I was energized and restored from within. I began to record my dream.

I hadn't studied dreams in any formal way, nor did I have an expert explain it to me. I'm going to give you the dreams as they came to me without a lot of stuff about what they meant. You can think about that for yourself. Much later in my journaling, I would seek out books about dreams like Carl Jung, MAN AND HIS SYMBOLS, or a book about interpreting objects. I had always dreamt a lot. I would journal my dreams for fourteen years and accumulate a big box full of dream notebooks. When I started that venture, I was married to my husband Ralph, and we lived in Fall City with our two daughters, Sasha nine and Sonia five.

Chapter Two

    I had already began to develop an interest in my dreams before I actually made the commitment to write them all down on April, 22 1974. I trusted the dream source because of a dream I had when our daughter Sasha was three. The dream caused me to wake up and saved my family's lives. We were living in Upper Preston in a sculptor's old cabin at the time. Ralph was attending Bellevue Community College in horticulture. I was working part time, hand dipping chocolates at Julius Boehm's Candy Kitchen, while Sasha was cared for by the lady from whom we bought our Rhode Island Red, brown chicken eggs. We had an old pot belly stove we burned coal in for heat. We all slept in a small attic.

    One night, I dream of a man standing near me watching my actions intently. I'm having trouble breathing. I cough and grasp my throat, because I can't seem to get enough air. This causes me such anxiety I waken.

    Our upstairs was filled with smoke! I shook my husband awake, and we grabbed Sasha from her sleep and rushed down the attic stairs into the living room. The whole house was consumed in smoke. Ralph had banked the fire, but turned down the damper too much on our coal burning stove. He opened the damper and we started airing out our cabin. We were very thankful to be alive. The man in my dream was watching over me to see what decision I would make.

I also found a pre-recorded dream, written on Feb. 2 of the same year I started recording my dreams. That one gave me the confidence to start this venture.

In this dream, I'm out on the Arctic tundra. The air is cold and fresh, and the ground rolling and stony. There is a thin layer of short, green grass peeking through. I have a few sheep entrusted to me that I'm to watch over and protect from the Arctic wolves. These wolves are large and hungry with ragged coats and sunken, desperate eyes. I'm aware I must work fast to devise a plan to save my sheep from being eaten, for the wolves are in our vicinity. Up ahead I see a huge pile of bones from around eighty sheep which were eaten the previous year. Their bones are bleached white and sticking up, as if they all died right where they stood, huddled together. At the sight of the bones, an idea comes to me. I'm excited! I have a plan. I hide my sheep in the middle of the pile, down among the bones. My sheep lie quietly as though they are asleep. I step back from the circle of bones.

Then, I see coming slowly toward me three or four wolves with their heads hung down sniffing for food. I feel confident and unafraid, but anxious for the wolves to move on by. They approach the bones and smell disinterestedly and continue around the pile. One wolf steps into the outer edge of dried bones. I say, "There's nothing there for you to eat." The wolf glances at me and slowly moves on.

Then I wakened, I thought, *Guess wolves don't eat clever shepherdesses.* When I was young, I had nightmares of running away from something that was scaring me. My sheep would have been lost then and I, chased within a gasp of my last breath. Although, in those dreams, I was always able to wake myself up before anything horrible happened, like choking on the smoke while my family slept in danger. Now, I've stopped being a victim! I've married and I'm taking responsibility for my life. It's good to have found one's strength and own way.

In my first week of journaling, I found myself standing in my dream in front of a fireplace. I'm saying a prayer to a group of people. I was shocked at recalling this. I didn't say prayers, let alone to a group. In short, the person who was myself in the dream was very different than how I was when awake. She was a self I didn't seem to know. She did things I didn't know how to do. Over the fourteen years I wrote in my journal, my dream self and my earthly self, started to come together. My whole life began to change.

I had some warning about these changes, as an astrologer at an arts and crafts fair gave me a mini reading. She said my entire life would be going through some major changes. I learned later, this was the time when planet Saturn would return to the spot where it was when I was born, the birthing aspect. I couldn't image what would change in my life, as we were comfortably settled on our tree farm. My husband Ralph had his goals in place with Raging River Nursery and Tree Farm, plus Green Earth Landscaping and Maintenance Company. It was a three-way partnership with two of his best friends. I'd built my jewelry and painting studio on our property with the help of my father and a good friend, who was the designer and building contractor. It's true I had trouble getting my studio permit because we lived in a flood zone. But since no one would be living in the studio and my neighbors hadn't objected, I finally succeeded. There, I was creating my handcrafted jewelry and painting my oil paintings. I even taught a children's art class. It looked like my husband and I were settled, and we had everything we wanted. But all was not as I hoped or as secure as I had imagined. Here was a dream preceding the building of my studio. It foretold some troubles I would encounter.

In the dream, I'm at a gift show where vendors are selling their work. People are lined up at these booths waiting to purchase the crafts. I dodge around some of the lines to get a peek at what is being sold. I'm surprised at what I see, because the items being bought are kind of corny and not made very well. My handcrafted jewelry is much better than that. I decide this show is not worth seeing, so I leave.

Now, I find myself in another room. I'm holding a cute little, roly-poly baby. I feel so over joyed and in love with this child. I play with the baby making funny faces and cooing at the infant. I snuggle and hold him close. It occurs to me the baby might be hungry. There's now a baby bottle of milk in my hands. I start to feed my child. As I do this, a matronly woman with gray hair and a pleasant face, appears and tells me I need to sterilize the bottle first so the baby doesn't get sick. She continues on about how I can't give the baby regular milk, but the baby needs a special formula. I don't seem to know about these things, so I decide to breast feed my baby. It's been a long time since I nursed my own children, so I'm not sure I still have any milk. I begin to nurse my baby anyway. I don't seem to have enough milk to satisfy my baby's hunger. I can feel my breast going dry from the strong sucking motion pulling through my whole body. This pull finally focuses on a lump under my skin on my lower left arm and begins to hurt. The matronly woman says, "You can't nurse the baby, because it might get an infection from you." I think the lump is probably an abscess. I feel a wave of intense sadness run through me. I might have to give up my child because I can't feed my baby.

Now, I'm in our red van with Ralph who is driving down the alley leaving the gift show. I'm holding my baby, and I know I'll have to go back to the gift show, but Ralph will disagree on the direction I want to travel. I'm very angry and say, "Let me out of the van. I will meet you back at the gift show." I take my child and walk around to the front of the block. Now the going gets difficult. The walkway goes through store fronts and I keep having to find the right way out. I come on a large red brick building with an aquarium show inside. I almost stop to see the show, but then remember Ralph will be waiting for me. My path takes me into a restaurant also made of red brick. People are eating lunch. The door I need to leave by is at the top of a wall near the ceiling, very strange. There is only a narrow brick ledge leading to my exit. I try balancing myself, as I slowly walk up it, but I need both hands. I can't do this, because I'm carrying my little baby. I back down again.

At a table near by me is a father, mother and a son eating lunch. I ask the tall dark father, "Will you hold my baby while I climb the wall to the door at the top, then hand me my child?" He agrees and lifts up my baby to me. I find myself back outside in the alley I had left in the first place, near our destination. (Boy, is it hard to go back twice to the same spot in a dream.) Unless you have an unresolved problem there.

As we walk down the alley, I'm threatened by a big black dog who dashes out at us snapping his jaws like he wants to bite us. When he reaches us, I grab him with my free hand by the nape of his neck and shove him along in front of us. I feel the baby is helping me. The dog, in a show of strength, is able to stop us. He then changes into a sheep that is again resisting us with all its might. We keep pushing forward in a steady motion. I know the game now. If the sheep is able to stop us, it might turn into a bigger animal, and we might not be able to control the forward progress. We might even have a monster, so I'm not going to let this sheep stop us!

I waken before anything else can happen. Have you ever wanted something so much you were willing to pursue it even if (in the end), you lost it? At least you had it for a short, wonderful time. Since, I've mentioned my studio (baby), I want to tell you about it. I was so proud of it. The structure was 24 feet square with a three foot decking all the way around it. It was built up on concrete pads, so it would be above the 100 year flood zone. I could walk all around the building enjoying the view. I dug the holes of the four foot square footings myself. Luckily, it was soft loam from years of the Raging River flooding onto the property. The river was on the other side of the highway and faced my building. The studio was built out of rough, cedar planking from a local saw mill. The shake roof had two skylights and there was a toilet closet. My father built my show case, counters and jewelry sink. We added a Franklin stove in one corner. Mr. Hawk hand carved my studio sign, the name "Soul Gems". There would be tourists on the highway to Snoqualmie Falls who might stop in. I had an intercom from the studio to the house for my kids to inform me when they were home from school. It also worked as a security system. I was in heaven. My own place to create the ideas that flowed through my mind. There were no interruptions to my deep thoughts, my quiet creation spot.

Chapter Three

As part of my changing focus of mind, I received in the mail some information about the Edgar Cayce Foundation and read about the Sleeping Prophet by Jess Stearn. This was a whole new kind of thought process for me. People began to tell me about books I should read. I made a rule if three people told me to read the same book, I would buy the book and read it, because it was meant for me. When "JONATHAN LIVINGSTON SEAGULL" flew in, I devoured Richard Bach's books, then Carlos Castaneda's books. These books began to show me the world was more illusory than I had thought.

I dream I'm in an art class. I recognize Barney, who my friend Pam is dating, plus an old friend of Ralph's, Andrew. The teacher is talking to us, but we can't see him. We just hear his voice. He is assigning material to us we each need to work on. My lesson is to study a large, beautifully stylized drawing of a tree. I study the picture of the full grown tree. It clearly shows the structure of how it grew. The tree is perfect with melodious lines that open like many cupped hands. The background moves easily through the tree as no lines completely enclose it. I'm to concentrate on the upper half of the tree where the larger, main branches stretch out from the trunk, to notice their relationship to the smaller tributaries extending out from them. I'm very amazed and awed by the drawing of the tree.

Another evening, I dream Ralph is molding his life after a beautiful oak tree. There were other symbols that portrayed his mission in life and direction he'd pursued, but I couldn't remember what it was, as though I wasn't supposed to know.

In the morning after I'd seen our girls off on their buses to school, I'd strolled through the tree farm to my studio to work. I'd stopped hoeing the weeds in the nursery, as Ralph brought in six white geese to keep the weeds down around the trees. I was free to design and paint whatever I wanted. I noticed Ralph was jealous of my building. He began to talk about constructing his own nursery office behind our house. I didn't think he really needed an office, since he mainly sold wholesale to places Green Earth was landscaping. But his ego did, and once he'd set his mind on something, there was no turning him back. For instance, the pond he'd dug in the back of our place where it was swampy. He planted it with fish, but the first flood took it all away.

His nursery office was modeled after my studio, built up out of the 100 year flood level. He didn't have the decking, but did have a sleeping loft. He had a long rectangular window that extended almost to the roof. He'd ask me to design a stained glass fir tree to fill the window. He took my scale drawing and had it built by a professional. It looked gorgeous installed.

I considered my husband to be a strong person. He was six feet two inches tall with an imposingly, large mustache. He was also very pushy about what he thought and wanted; Aries. His attitude was constantly creating problems for me.

I dream I'm taking a jewelry class, my area of study. The teacher of the class turns out to be my husband Ralph. He seems rather unsure of this subject. He starts his presentation with a lot of math. I think, "*Oh, no, I'm not very good at this kind of logic. Ralph knows more about math than I do.*" Ralph writes down on the chalkboard two fractions which he is going to explain to us how to solve, but he stops because the denominators are different. As I look at the fractions, I realize this problem is easy. They both reduce to ½. If you add them together you get one whole, like two people in a relationship. One is not greater than the other.

I began to have ideas about how things should be, rather than how they were, as shown in the next dream. In it, my bedroom is in a tower connected to our house. I'm up in the bedroom with my two daughters Sasha and Sonia who were young. It is cozy, warm and bright like being inside my childhood dollhouse. Through a small window, I can look out and see for miles. We are very content and happy. It's time to go down the stairs to the main house. I open the door and look down the small spiral chamber with highly polished wooden stairs curving around the tower. The wall side of the stairs are wide and the inside of the steps lead to a point. We walk down very carefully.

When we are inside the main house, a man tells me. "It's too, much trouble to have bedrooms way upstairs like that, you'd always be running back and forth."

I reply, "It's no trouble. We only go there when we wish to sleep."

In my waking thoughts, I realized I was looking for a safe place to rest from relationship craziness. There I could just enjoy my girls and our quiet space. No interference.

I found in my dreams, the action and landscapes were always changing. I seemed to accept that in the dream realm. I became a true explorer. I didn't question the circumstances, but I did have to deal with what was before me, which could be anything you might imagine and more, as you will see in my dreams. Running away didn't work well, because I would be chased causing a lot of hard breathing. I've found it's better to stand and face the problem with all your courage. Then it will dissolve before your frightened eyes into something more manageable. When you truly understand something doesn't work, you won't resort to it.

Sometimes my dreams were fun, like being in Pasco where I grew up. In this dream, I'm at my childhood park by my favorite tall slide with three bumps. I smile as my eyes sweep the slide. Then I notice at the far corner of the park, a red brick building that seems to be an apartment house. The building is done in a Spanish style with two full length arched, paned windows on each side of a double door. There are three of these apartments connected to each other. Each has a small concrete patio in front of its doors along the sidewalk. The glass inside the door and windows of the middle apartment are a beautiful shade of blue. I wonder what it would be like to live there with the lovely blue light streaming in on my inner world.

There seems to be no one around to hamper my curiosity and the apartments are quiet, so I walk over. Now, I find there are two buildings. I can walk between them. As I do this, I see a side window to look through. I discover the building on my left has a vacant living room, except for a number of empty bird cages all in different sizes and shapes. I wonder if someone is going to sell bird cages, but here is no sign of this. I decide to see if I can find the birdcage I like the best. I don't see what I'm looking for, so I turn and walk across the narrow space between the apartments and look into the other one's window.

It's the same. The room is full of more different stylized cages. After studying the cages, I do see my favorite one. It's sitting near the window I'm peering through. The cage is made of white porcelain with a bas-relief floral design scrolled around the bottom of the cage. It is dome shape. There's a perch rising from the cage floor to about mid-way to center, where a bird could sit above the porcelain bottom and look out, as though she were in the center of a little stage about to sing an operatic aria. I feel pleased to have found my favorite birdcage, my stage in life.

On considering the dream, I was a trapped bird. I could sing about anything creative that brought me joy and happiness. I loved using my own ideas and making my designs on things, or through them. Someday, I'll fly free from the bars of learned limitations. I knew there was a way through my own self-inflicted fears. I would have to remove them one by one as I learned a better way to fly.

Chapter Four

As a kid I enjoyed having fairytales read to me, there, anything was possible like dreams. However, there were rules of behavior that moved you forward or sent you to prison. I could shut the book if I didn't like the story. If a dream was too tough, I could cry myself awake. My Mommy told me dreams where not real. But they seemed real to me, though I was very glad when scary ones were gone. In dreams everything I saw was real to me, and I reacted to it. Here is one of my adult fairytales.

I'm in a different land than I've ever seen before. It has a low overgrown forest along a shoreline with some islands nearby. The trees are not very tall, and there's a lot of light in the forest. I walk along the shore through the bushes, then I come to a clearing with a large abandoned, wooden house. It has cracked and peeling white paint. I stop, but I have no wish to go toward this house.

I turn away and continue along the shore. Then a voice from above me says, "The abandoned house is the dwelling place of a mean witch and her magical monster. They have captured a person and are holding this person prisoner. You should help free this person." I ponder this choice. To help someone escape from something they don't want, is a brave choice. I decide to take the task.

In a minds flash, I travel to a monastery in a faraway place. I stand before a monk of great knowledge. I ask him how I can drive out the evil witch from the house to save the person trapped within.

He tells me now would be a good time to do this for the witch is gone on business from the house. This should make it easier for me. I thank him and immediately, I'm back where I first saw the house.

It is so, the witch's house seems abandoned but I wonder where her magical monster is? I'm afraid he might be watching the house in some way. I go through the front door and walk toward the back of the house. I come onto a balcony overlooking a stone dungeon that is in the basement. I can see the layout of the compartmental stone rooms, as though there is no roof. There are stairs down, and a passageway along the rooms.

I decide to go down the stairs and find the trapped prisoner in one of the stone cells. I see the captive. I'm shocked, for it's my own six year old daughter Sonia! I grab her tightly by the hand. She wipes away her tears, as we hastily ascend the stone stairs and go back out of the house the same way I came in.

Outside, I tell her we must hurry and get as far away from the house as possible. I know I must watch out for the magical monster who guards the house. We are lucky we haven't run into him so far. Hand-in-hand, we sneak off for the shoreline to head up the coast.

As we come down near the water, I notice from one of the nearby islands, a force of sparks launch out from there into the bay traveling straight toward us. I know it's the monster coming! The sparks blow the water in a shimmering manner, as it moves across the ocean.

Fear fills me, and we flee as fast as we can, but the force is gaining on us. Now, we are scrambling on hands and knees through the dirt and undergrowth and up the side of the hill. The force has reached land and is coming after us, shaking the bushes as it comes. It's quite close!

Then I see green cucumbers growing on the ground around us. I pick one up and throw it at the force, saying "Go away evil monster!" The cucumber misses. I quickly throw another, but the same thing happens again. I realize I need more power. The Force is not turning away, but is almost to us.

I say, "Sonia, say go away evil monster!" We say it together and I throw another cucumber. This time it hits the force. It immediately disappears.

I wakened very spooked after the dream. I don't like evil magic. Who controls that magic? I know now, it wasn't real but I had to stand up to what I thought was real in the dream. Because Sonia was being saved too, she had to participate in its demise. I learned the power of two people working together! I couldn't save her, unless she wanted to be saved and helped me. We are all in the world together. Let's help one another towards our highest good.

Sometimes in dreams, I'm reminded of things I thought I couldn't do well. Here is one of those dreams. I'm in college sitting by myself in a library studying a drawing. An older man comes by with another college student, a young woman. They stop in front of me and start talking to me. The woman is very happy about what she has learned and wants to share with me. She begins pronouncing some large, difficult words. Then she shows me how she's learned to speak in foreign languages.

I say, "That's very good. Big words and foreign languages are not what I'm good at. I'm working on feelings and the understanding of life."

On waking, I thought perhaps the tall, dark man and student could teach me these things, if I gave up my ideas I'm not good at it. I needed to stay open to all learning experiences and leave my judgments about my abilities out of it. Who knows what I might need to learn?

Another thought drifted in, "Do not criticize others, for if you truly have control and direction over yourself, you will not need to prove it by manipulating and directing others. Help, if it is asked of you, but try to see their point of view, not yours."

Chapter Five

While living in Fall City my husband and I met Bob at a grade school P.T.A. meeting. We all instantly liked each other. Bob, a small, dark haired man, had a wife and five kids. He was a veterinarian and had a receptionist named Pam. We met her when we took our cat in for treatment. Pam invited us all over to her forest home, except for Bob's wife, who didn't like Pam. I learned Bob and Pam were involved in an affair and Bob's wife got wind of it. Pam was divorced from her husband who made big bucks. Their son and daughter were living with her.

At Pam's house, she tested me with a childhood game of hand clapping back and forth. As we laughed, I never missed a beat. We became good friends after that test. I liked her fiery energy and the way she always seemed to get to the bottom of debates. She was gregarious, short, with large breasts, the oldest of four sisters.

Pam complained a lot to me about her second sister, Jackie's relationship problems. I met Jackie at Pam's house. I had problems too, with my husband.

I dream I'm with Jackie and we are going to school again enrolled in the first grade. I'm sitting in my tiny chair at my table with some other children. I see Jackie sitting at another table. Our bodies are full size, way larger than the other kids. I wait for my lessons.

The teacher leaves to talk to the principal in his office about us. All the classrooms have intercom systems and there are no secrets kept from the students. We can hear their conversation on the intercom. A loud argument breaks out over the speaker between the principal and our teacher.

I think, *how will I learn anything with that disruption going on?* Our teacher comes back, and Jackie and I are assigned to the fifth grade. I'm glad and think to myself the math will be more interesting there.

The dream suggested to me, in our early years, Jackie and I didn't learn the right lessons. I guess we needed to relearn what we had not learned correctly. My belief system was in need of an overhaul. I was operating on a premise or premises that didn't work.

As disturbing problems came up for me in my relationship with my husband, I decided to take that wild energy and channel it into poems. I tried to make some sense out of my feelings and life, to find some resolution. Poetry was something my husband Ralph loved in his college years. He had collected some books of his favorite writers and wrote poems himself. I hadn't cared for some of these writers. I wanted him to write more, though he hadn't chosen that direction. He still thought of himself as the poet expert of the family and so criticized my work. I felt sad, but I couldn't let myself be stopped in my projects because of his judgments. I wouldn't share much with those who were critical of me. It doesn't encourage me to go forward, unless he could show me a better way that would help. Much later, Ralph confessed he was just jealous of my writing. I considered myself a visual artist, and Ralph argued I was excluding him from my artist category. I had since decided all people are artist of their own lives. They perhaps don't realize how much they use their own minds with their fears, hopes and dreams to create what happens to them. We do need to watch what we're asking for, because nothing comes to us without our bidding, so I've been told by THE COURSE IN MIRACLES by the Foundation For Inner Peace. Here is one of my older poems written on May 17, 1976.

KIRAYA KESTIN

LOOKING

I'm looking for that part of me
that grows tall and green,
from roots buried deep within,
hidden, yet glimpsed in dreams,
attached and layered
in a soil of earthy toil.
I don't want to be influenced
or broken by the wind,
shaded or crowded out by others.
I'm looking for that part of me
that can endure,
producing lush flowers and succulent fruit.
I see transparent layers, superimposed on one spot;
all the directions I've chosen in one shot.
There must be hundreds of ME's.
Yet, they rose from one source,
to recalculate the course.
It is my center, not the outside force.
My center anchors me,
holds me to my ground
through all kinds of gale.
The part of me, forever rising
calmly out of the earth,
to begin again as new growth,
nourished by the seed of the inner me.

Chapter Six

I wanted to learn what worked in my relationship with Ralph. When I married I thought my husband shared similar values with me, but that was sometimes far from the truth. I kept bumping into glaring differences in the rules of our relationship that needed to be addressed. I was pretty conventional in what I thought marriage was about. The next dream showed one of my typical problems.

I'm shopping with Ralph inside a large mall. Ralph loses interest and wanders off. I find an import shop, and I'm looking at the different artifacts for sale. I come to some Japanese lanterns you could hang from your ceiling over a light bulb. I'm fascinated. I want to buy one. I hold up a white, pleated paper lantern. It changes shape. Instead of being small and round, it has two large appendages and are almost as tall as I am. Both appendages are joined at the top, like a pair of lungs. I find this very strange, and I'm not sure how I would use it. I decide not to buy it.

I go looking for Ralph. I find him talking to a woman he has met. He introduces me to his friend, and starts telling me how much he's been enjoying her. I'm patient, but not very interested in hearing about his new woman friend. I say, "I'd like to leave now, so could you say your goodbyes." I can see Ralph is having a hard time deciding if he wants to go leaving his dark haired lady friend behind.

Ralph says to me, "I want to walk her back to her apartment first." This seems reasonable to me, but I'm coming along. We all stroll along to her apartment which is in this same building. I'm friendly to a point, but I don't want to get involved with this woman.

We arrive at her door and bid her goodbye. She closes the door behind her and we start to walk down the hall. Then Ralph stops, and starts to tell me something about this woman. Just then, the woman opens her door and comes back down the hall toward us. She is wearing a V neck dress open all the way to her waist. Her bra is showing across her front. I know she is trying to entice my husband into not leaving.

I think to myself. *If you're going to wear a dress like that, at least have enough sense to take off your bra!*

Ralph turns to me and says, "Didn't I tell you she's a neat chick! Look at the way she dresses." The woman takes hold of Ralph's hand and motions, while pulling him toward her apartment. Then she lets go and continues towards her door. I beginning to get pissed off, and I'm not about to leave! I follow Ralph right into her bedroom. There she is lying on her bed with her dress top pulled down, showing her bra and trying to look appealing.

Ralph is really intrigued. He goes right over to her. I'm fast reaching boiling point! I say, "Very sexy. You might at least shown him your nipples." So she pries one out.

Mesmerized, Ralph lowers his lips towards her wrinkled boob. That's it. I have had it. I'm furious! I yell, "I'm leaving this place right now, and I'm not coming back!" I storm to the door. Ralph seems drunk, but staggers after me.

In the hall I turn and shout something else at him. There's a white Styrofoam cup full of crushed ice in my hand. I throw it at him giving him an ice shower. (I would actually do this very thing later on in our lives!)

Now we are back in our red van, and I'm angrily driving away from this building on a makeshift road that leads around the building to the main road. There seems to be a lot of excavating going on around this building. The roads are sketchy and not clear. I turn down one road, to find I should have gone the other way, so I go back to head in the right direction.

Then I see my girls running over the dirt mounds, calling out, "Wait for us!" The delay is irritating to me and I will, of course, not leave without them. I notice big machinery on the scene, a huge bulldozer and a loader. I get out of the van and come around to the right side of the road to warn Sonia not to run in front of the bulldozer's path.

Sasha stops, but all Sonia can think of is getting to us. The bulldozer is moving back and forth. The blade pushes her right into the soft dirt as it passes over her. I'm horrified! I yell, "Stop, stop", at the dozer! I beat my fists on the huge blade. The driver sees me and stops.

I can see some of Sonia's yellow dress sticking up out of the dirt where she went down. I rush for the spot, heart in my mouth. I dig and pull Sonia up into my arms. I cry out, "Sonia are you alright!" Her body seems alive. I hold her back from me to get a look at her face, for she hasn't answered me. I see her nose and mouth are full of dirt. I quickly clear the dirt away so she can breathe again.

I woke up thanking God for Sonia's safety! I realized children can get hurt by parents' conflicts. I've had these kinds of women problems with Ralph over and over again. When I hadn't notice his wanderings, he'd come and confess to me like I was some sort of priest. What was I to do once he felt clean again? I told him we were going to have an open marriage. I'm going to have men friends, too. Ralph had a harder time with my friends than I had with his. Probably, because I was pickier, and he had to baby sit. But I had my dreams to deal with and this is what happened.

I fall asleep dreaming of being in a big bed with Ralph on my left side, and my two daughters on my right side. Something is bothering my sleep. I open my eyes to see what it might be. This thing has crawled across my neck, and I feel a large, long round body lying between Ralph and me.

Our girls have gone. I'm frozen with fear, for I'm sure it's a huge snake! I want to find out if I'm right, but I'm afraid to move in this very dark room. I, very lightly run my hand over the long body. Yes, it's a big fat snake, and I sense the rest of its body is coiled by my head on my pillow to the left side of me! This is dangerous. I need to save myself.

I think of alerting Ralph to help, but the sound of my voice might awaken the sleeping snake. I want so much to call out to him, but I decide to keep my advantage over the reptile. This snake has to go!

My plan is to quickly sit up and at the same time throw the snake out of bed. This I do, but the snake is apparently waiting for me to make my move. It swings its head quickly around sinking it's fangs into my lower left arm! I'm temporarily overcome by a great numbing pain from his bite.

I can see the snake clearly, now. Its head is as big as my fist, and the body as thick as a leg. It's an Anaconda water snake with green and yellow round spots. It's lazy and slow moving, a lover of warmth, but a crushing opponent! With my right hand, I seize the snake by the back of its head away from its mouth. I know to have control over the snake, I must have its head. To kill the snake, I must destroy the head.

Applying as much pressure as I can to the base of the snake's head, I lift its teeth and head off my left arm. I jump out of bed dragging the snake behind me, and go toward the kitchen to find a big knife, or something to destroy the snake's head. I'm in a combination kitchen living room, but I can't seem to lay my hands on a lethal instrument to use against the snake.

I'm surprised that my own strength remains strong. Then I notice juices are coming out of the snake's mouth. I move the snake's head all around, so its own juices are all over its head. The Anaconda's head shrivels up to a dried stump before my very eyes! I'm amazed. Relief is slow to come and I decide it would be okay to lay the heavy, dead body down for it will do no more harm without a head to direct it.

When I woke up and processed the dream, I thought it was about dealing with sexual temptations. An open marriage wasn't going to work for me, even if it was the time of the Flower Children and changing values and roles. It was Ralph's double standard I didn't want. I could stop it, kill it at its source, but Ralph didn't seem to want to do that. We don't make the rules. A higher power did that long ago. Truth never changes, we think we can play around with it. I'd walk the straight and narrow, if it kept a snake out of my bed, but that was hindsight. I'd rather not sleep if I had to deal with that stuff. I should have been glad I wasn't killed, but there was no real death in dreams, just endings. I saved myself! I've seen people killed in dreams, who then, got up and walked off. What a relief that was!

Because Ralph and I were having so many troubles with his behavior and my values, Ralph's father recommended we go to the psychiatrist he had seen after his divorce from Ralph's mother. After both of us met with the doctor, he told me that "Ralph wants hot, cold ice cream. It doesn't exist." The psychiatrist said, he thought he could work better with me to understanding Ralph's cycles.

Another problem in our relationship stemmed from my thinking I should listen to all Ralph's troubles. I guess I thought it worth sharing, but it was depressing to hear. After a bit, I just wanted to fix it all, so I didn't have to hear it again. Now I've learned the bad news wasn't worth sharing. It was full of personal fear, which was fabricated. Who would want to hear it anyway? *Make it short. Shit does happen! The bigger you make it, the harder it will be to forgive. I can't save you. You need to save yourself.* But, I didn't know that at the time. I was always trying to save him from all the troubles he'd gotten himself into. I worried when he was not happy, as though it was my job to make him happy.

Years later, I learned from the THE COURSE IN MIRACLES book that the point of relationships was "to make happy". I was trying to do that, but what was Ralph doing? At that time in my life, I still felt I had to get people to love me, or I didn't have any love. This turned out to be one of my main problems.

Chapter Seven

In my reading I came across the idea we've lived past lives and have brought past karma into our present lives to work out. Sometimes I'm shown dreams I thought were about my past lives because of the settings and thought systems. When that happens, I'm with a guide who leads me during sleep.

We are back in time at the Roman period. It's during the killing of Christians. I see a large, round stone building like a coliseum. This building is full of captive Christians. The Roman army is guarding these people, while waiting for a verdict from high officials as to the fate of these helpless souls. Death is declared. Every one of these people will be systematically killed. I feel horror for the soldiers who will have to wade through the bodies slinging their swords in this useless slaughter of lives, not to mention the Christians who will die. My narrator says, "And these bodies of the Jews will be boiled and their oil will be used to oil the Roman's roads."

I thought the word "Jew" was interesting here. Perhaps, the Romans in power at that time became reincarnated Nazis and the Christians, Jews. I wasn't sure why I was shown that, perhaps the cycle of cruelty that continues in our world waiting for forgiveness and for mankind to make different choices, one for love and freedom. Where was our brotherhood? Perhaps, the past and possible future can be viewed with guides at any time, because everything is happening at the same time or no time. Perhaps time was only an earthly structure?

Here is another example of a past life dream. I find myself in a large, what must be an ancient room built from huge cut stones. I have a narrator with me who is explaining to me what is happening. I'm not in a body, but sort of a transparent image. I see a gathering of men all dressed alike. Their chests are bare to their waists and they have smooth, dark yellow-pink skin. Their hair length is straight and black at shoulder length, but curls up slightly at the ends. Goatees are on their chins. They wear matching upper arm bracelets with a black curling design and have belted, white skirts down to their sandals.

Some of the men are waiting on an overweight, older man who seems to be their leader. A ritual is being performed. One of the men hands their leader a long sword. He is going to commit a kind of hari-kari and kill himself. All the men look sad but determined this should happen.

The narrator says, "There's a curse on the land and their leader is preforming this ritual to counteract the curse." Some of the other men are grouped to one side trying to determine what should be done next. I become scared that this might have something to do with me!

I waken quickly, feeling quite spooked and afraid about that event. I wasn't sure what to do with this kind of dream. Was I part of their belief system life, and carried some locked in fear? I thought of Carlos Castaneda's book THE TEACHING OF DON JUAN: A YAQUI WAY OF KNOWLEDGE. In it, Don Juan had said some of the ancient, dark belief systems hang out around ruins or places they were practiced long ago. They don't go away. The beliefs can try to attach to you and cause you trouble. He says to stay away, or carry a prayer of protection.

Later in my story, I will share a past life dream I know links to my progress on earth.

I hadn't been getting enough sleep lately, so I'd been sleeping more deeply. This causes the recalling of my dreams to be harder. I felt like a stone plunging to the bottom of a lake. I was learning that it was quite necessary to keep in touch with one's energies and needs, so balance can be maintained. The flow between daily events and the spiritual dream world needed to remain balanced and open. Then the spiritual self could get on with the teaching of our progressing selves, instead of having to spend time on pointing out destructive behavior in our daily lives.

Chapter Eight

While Ralph and I were trying to work out our marital problems, we met a man named Leonard, who did twenty-four hour group therapy marathons. Our friend Bob and his wife had done some counseling with him. They recommended him to us. We tried his group therapy.

In the wee hours of the morning, when our defenses were down, it was amazing what tumbled out of my mouth. The process helped me feel closer to others in a safe group. I realized, I was feeling, too separated and cut off in my body. I wasn't sharing my love as much as I could. We did a number of these sessions. I discovered I had some childhood pain I blocked off from myself.

In 2014, I put that story in my book "REMEMBER ME" which I'd self-published. I found writing the book to be a very healing process. I felt happiness when I read my book.

Here is a dream where Ralph's sister Betty is working in a dry cleaning shop. She suggests Ralph and I get remarried. We talk this over between us and find it an exciting thing to do.

We travel to an old gothic church. A priest opens the door dressed in his ceremonial robe. He sweeps his arm in the direction we're to go. We enter a dimly lit room with tables for two scattered around the room. Each table has a red glass, candle holder with a candle burning in it. The room feels cozy and intimate, even though the ceiling must be very high. We pick a table in the center of the hall and sit across from each other. I notice there are more couples at other tables. We are to stay at these tables for 24 hours, and then the ceremony would be finished. Every so often little bites of food are brought to us. It's alright to talk quietly together of our relationship and love for each other.

This dream did reflect what was happening for us at the time. Our relationship began to improve. Ralph was more supportive and helpful. We decided to reenact our wedding vows during the spring. We planned a fun wedding at Seattle Arboretum when the cherry blossoms would be in full bloom. I made for myself and our two daughters granny dresses to wear at the event. Mine had a white apron, and I wore a flowered wreath in my hair. I also made Ralph's shirt in dark green with white flowers. We had a wonderful loving event! We had hired a photographer to take action pictures of our party.

Later, in my studio, I painted an oil painting of Ralph and me from one of the photos taken at our wedding. Our relationship was good for a while. Unfortunately, we began to slide into old habits and fears. Our past problems began to return. I didn't know how to stop that from happening.

The next dream pointed to this change.

I'm inside our home in Fall City. I go into my daughter Sasha's bedroom. I look up and notice the attic door is open. I can see through the open hatch the inside of the roof and beams. There's a red glow coming from the edges of one of the beams that supports our roof. It's a fire smoldering and hot! I feel the danger. I must do something quick to get the fire out before it bursts into flames and destroys our home.

Hurriedly, I leave Sasha's bedroom to warn the family. But once out of the room, I forget what I saw. Sometime later, an errand takes me back into Sasha's bedroom. I look up again and see the smoldering fire. I'd forgotten about it! I feel awful, because the fire has spread from the beam to the roof, making a large red glowing circle. I know when we put out the fire the wood fiber will be destroyed creating a large hole in our roof. Still, the fire hasn't burst into flames, so maybe there's a little more time. Also, a strange thing, there is no smoke.

I rush out of the bedroom to the kitchen where Ralph is working at the sink. I frantically tell him, "The attic is on fire and we must put it out quickly!" Ralph doesn't seem to be very interested and moves slowly off. I grab him and demand he do something about the fire. I say, "I'll get some water. You go get the ladder from the shed."

Ralph wanders out the backdoor. I hurry to the sink and start pouring water into whatever I find. I'm very upset as I carry a bucket and two glasses of water into Sasha's bedroom where I set them on the floor for Ralph. He comes in without the ladder.

I say "Why didn't you bring the ladder? We must hurry!" Ralph looks up at the large smoldering fire. I just can't stand it. "I'll bring a hose through the bedroom window," I say. Ralph insists I use the front door, instead. I don't argue, but rush out and come back with the garden hose.

This time, I find Ralph standing on the ladder ready to receive the hose. I quickly pass it to him. He begins to spray the fire. I nervously stand there wondering if I should call the fire department to back us up in case we can't get the fire out. I feel embarrassed about letting the fire department know we have a fire, so I don't call. I wait to see how Ralph is doing fighting the fire.

Pretty soon, Ralph calls down that the fire is out. I'm so relieved. We all creep up into the attic to have an inspection. There is no sign of any fire being there at all, no blackness. I feel the beam in disbelief. I'm suspicious of the quick disappearance. We must watch the attic for any sparks inside the timber that would rekindle.

It seemed I wasn't getting much awareness from Ralph about problems that could ruin our marriage. I kept trying to make adjustments around some of Ralph's ideas about women friends. Why did he need to try and seduce women, any woman?

I decided to try automatic hand writing. I learned about it from a book I read. I wanted to see if it would reveal anything. Accordingly, I sat in a comfortable, quiet place with a piece of paper. I held the pencil lightly up right on the paper. I asked my question and wait for my hand to be guided.

I was told Ralph and I were lost. Ralph didn't believe he was loveable, so he tried to prove it by getting other women in bed. I didn't count, because I was his wife. He wouldn't be able to change his belief system in that way.

As I was resting quietly, I also heard a voice say, "In your later years, you will write a book about dreams." I was surprised, that sounded like a big project that I knew nothing about! I hadn't realized then, but my dream journaling was the start of my book, "DREAMING INSIDE OUT". I'm now writing it at age seventy.

Chapter Nine

Ralph and I met a couple of men doing personal growth seminars. We took some classes using meditation techniques. There I discovered (after I'd set aside my fear) and took a deep look into myself, that I'm not something awful but a beautiful loving soul.

In my journal, it was Sunday, September 1, 1974, and there's a full moon in Pisces. Now my dreams took a surprising turn. I seem to be in a large hotel. I'm passing through a big banquet room filled with tables covered in white tablecloths. I'm with two professional men, who I think are putting on a seminar in the basement of this building. I'm feeling in a good mood, so I jokingly pretend to snatch a wine bottle off the back table.

We seem to be in a hurry, or late and pass quickly through the building to the basement. In the basement some people are sitting in chairs placed against the wall. I move behind a small table covered with a white tablecloth and stand beside one of the professional speakers who will be addressing the group. A woman reporter is standing in front of us. She wants to interview my friend before we get started.

All of a sudden, I make a prediction of something that is going to happen. It surprises me, and I wonder why I said that. But I can't remember what I said.

The lady reporter turns to me and says, "Oh, so you make predictions. Have you ever done this before?"

I say, "No."

She is taking notes and says, "What sign are you?"

I answer, "Pisces." *I'm still feeling confused. I'm trying to figure out what's going on with me.* Then I collapse in a faint on the floor. My eyes are open. I can hear everything going on around me, but I'm unable to move or speak to reassure people I'm not sick.

People rush around me, feeling and checking my body signs. I'm caught in such a strong sensation I'm completely overwhelmed. It's not uncomfortable, just very intense. Then, I notice my body is rising off the ground and the people are trying to hold me down. I decide I must try to get control of myself. I sort of stiffen and then relax.

I say, "I'm all right," and I fly right out from under the people and straight up to the ceiling. There's beautiful music all around me. I feel so elated, as if the heavens have opened unto me. I stretch out my arms to all the people below me like I'm giving God's blessings to them. I know I'm not God, but I must be experiencing some of His glory. All the people are watching me in amazement and disbelief as I fly around the room. I playfully perform a couple of slow motion flips like underwater ballet.

When I land, two of my friends come up to me to question me about my experience. As I talk to them, I notice a red flash coming from the ceiling where the chimney ascends. I sense the red flash means danger or a stress area. I wonder if this ability to see this phenomenon is left over from the experience I just had of flying.

I excuse myself to go see if my perception is correct. I follow a stairway around the chimney up to the next floor. I see that the floor is receding from the chimney and is unstable. I turn and find my friends have followed behind me and are now in some danger. The stairs going down lead around this same chimney. I'm not sure how I will handle this situation.

I awaken. *Wow… a taste of heaven: only, love, joy and peace there! Where did that happen?* Inside of me, but there seemed to be some warning of weakness. I should develop a better structure to use that power. I was coming to some greater understanding here. It would take until the passing of both of my parents in 2008, within 26 hours of each other, before I would truly know heaven was inside of me.

Here's how it happened, I was driving my car down Aurora Avenue when I saw in my mind's eye, my deceased mother and father floating before me. They were in their twenties happily smiling at me as they drifted through space, safe and sound. I now knew where they were and where to look for them if I wanted to see them again, INSIDE ME.

When my mother was in hospice, I told her that after she passed away, she could come and see me in my dreams. She was surprised this was possible, but I reassured her it was true. I'd seen some of my other deceased relatives before in dreams.

One week after her passing, I dreamed of her. In my dream, I see a man with my mother. He says, "There she is," and points at me. Mother comes over and gives me a big hug! She feels as real as any live person! It was our closure. I'd given her my permission to do this and she did. Amen.

Another similar funny thing happen later in 2012, when I was writing my second book called REMEMBERING ME. In the chapter called "I Want Daddy", I revealed my true reason for running away to my father's workplace. It was to get a big hug from him. After I'd written this, my father came to me in a dream to give me the big hug I always wanted from him. I was up at our cabin in Birch Bay at the time. It is amazing to me how transparent heaven and earth really are.

Chapter Ten

Our friend Bob came over to our house to help Ralph and another workman fix our shed roof. I stood outside watching them. I noticed Bob was working twice as fast as the others. When Bob climbed off the roof, I said to him, "You don't have to work so hard just because you're of small stature." Bob immediately got angry. Ralph came over to see what the fuss was about and sided with him. I knew my friends didn't like me pointing out some of their faults. It wasn't my business, but sometimes their behaviors got in the way of my enjoying them. Now if it hadn't hit home, I guess it wouldn't have bothered Bob. It was that very incident that led to my first enlightenment outside of a dream.

I was taking a bath in our claw foot bathtub, crying because Bob and Ralph were mad at me. I felt no one understood me! Suddenly, an energy lifted me right up out of the bathtub to a place where a robed, white bearded man sat on a stone bench. I crawled over and put my head in his lap. I sobbed to him, I'm trying to do this and trying to do that. He stroked my head and said, "There's nothing you need to do. I only want your happiness."

Back in the bath tub again, I felt elated! If I did the things that made me happy, I would become light and rise up to him. I told my husband about this amazing experience.

He saw how happy I was. Ralph said, "Don't leave me behind."

I wondered who that bearded man was. Was he God or Moses? No one's supposed to be able to see God, but God could appear in any form he wanted. A loving father was a great form!

Now I had a different problem, because when trouble came up in the family concerning my relationships, I could see the bearded man smiling at me from above. I felt guilty if I was angry and didn't know what to do. I seemed to have two selves, one that was kind and another who was angry and acted out. Which was me, both of them? After a few more times of feeling guilty, I ask the man on high to go further away.

Here is a dream that points to this kind of problem. I'm standing at the top of a grand, old fashioned staircase in a mansion. I want to go down the stairs to join my family in the living room, but something is wrong with my eyes. I can hardly see. I rub my eyes and try to hold them open. I know I'm not blind, but something is causing my problem. Finally, after much struggle, I get my eyes to function well enough to see the stairs ahead of me. As I start down, a ghostly white form descends ahead of me. He turns his cold hearted eyes on me and says, "You're not going down stairs. I'll take care of your family for you."

He looks so evil and monstrous, I know he'll try to kill them. I reply, "You shall not harm my family. I will destroy you first!" I grab a long pole with a jagged end like a broken jousting lance. Even with my foggy eyesight, I ram it through the center of this spirit. The ghost groans and fades away, but his evil self-jumps from him into me. I hear his laughter echo inside me. I'm horrified, but I don't know what to do about this.

I go on down the stairs to greet my family and friends. As I talk to them, everyone seems fine. I notice there's a raging fire in the fireplace. It looks out of control and too hot for the chimney. My younger daughter Sonia wanders over to the fireplace out of curiosity. I urgently call to her to move away from the dangerous fire.

We all decide to leave the mansion. We go upstairs to get our things. I begin to have a strong need to tell someone about the devil spirit inside me. As we approach the stairs again, I anxiously pull my friends aside and tell them about the devil spirit that jumped inside of me. I say, "I have to get him out!" They don't seem to believe me. So I open my mouth as wide as I can, so they can see the devil inside. I look down my own throat with the others. I see and hear the devil's gruff, hallow laugh. Again, my friends still think I'm okay and there's nothing wrong with me. So if they aren't worried about me, I guess I'll let it go.

I pondered the dream. Was there evil inside of me? I knew when I thought of myself as a body, all my fears rose up to take form. I couldn't see correctly. In the dream, my friends thought I was okay and hadn't found anything wrong with me: because that was the human predicament. But I knew something was wrong. This was not who God created me to be!

What I really needed was in the works, because A COURSE IN MIRACLES was being born. I would find the book some years later at Unity Church. It would clearly show me my two selves, one that was the real Holy Spirit side, the other one fake, the ego, causing the split self. I would learn lessons in truth and take the Course in Miracles classes. I was raised on false beliefs that needed to be changed. I had a body, where fear liked to hang out, and I would have to deal with my ego, which could be an awesome tricky force. I knew fear would lead me wrong. How could I remember to follow my real voice? For now I was lost.

I continued to struggle, trying to managing my husband's problems. I guessed it was my way to avoid looking at myself and what I wanted. I found myself in this dream.

I'm standing on the bank of a waterfront at dusk. I look across the water at some boat docks. My eye catches the movement of some men pulling a large bag down to the end of one of the docks. They open the bag and dump out a man. I recognize him as my husband! They quickly cut off his head and dump his body into the water taking his head with them.

I feel shocked and outraged! They can't have Ralph's head. I must get it back. I know which way they went. I can follow them, but the men are dangerous. I'm going to need some help. I look around. I see a man with a knife and a street kid with a club. I ask them if they will go with me to get my husband's head back. They nod their willingness to accompany me on my mission.

Our group looks rather ragamuffin, but I lead the way. We start in the direction of the head-robbers. Though they have disappeared, I sense the way. After a short walk, the landscape has gone. There's only whiteness. I see a soldier standing to my right at attention with an automatic rifle at his side. Only his eyes track me as we approach. We are way overpowered, but he doesn't move a muscle. I guess we're not a threat, so I continue past him. A little further on is another sentinel, only this time, he's on my left. The same thing happens as with the first soldier. He doesn't move to stop us.

We travel forward weaving through this guarded pathway, until I see a large conference table up ahead. There are three men talking while bending over a large map. As we approach, the man at the head of the table looks up at me. He's wearing a business suit, but where his body should be, there is only glowing, golden light streaming out. No face, just light. He says to me, "I admire your fighting courage." He walks up to me and gives me a big hug. His touch is the most wonderful, comforting feeling I've ever felt! I'm elated and feel blessed. Nothing else matters to me anymore, but this. All my concerns disappear.

As I thought later about the dream, I realized the only person I could save was myself. Ralph would have to do his own spiritual work if he wanted to know who he really was. I would have to keep going wherever it led me. I had the strength and I was working on raising my consciousness, as shows in this next dream.

I find myself following a small path to the top of a high mountain. When I reach the top, I look around at the gorgeous view and wonder what I'm supposed to do here? Then a strong wind blows me right off the mountain! I'm totally surprised, but I remember I can fly so I glide down thousands of feet and find a safe place to land.

When I wrote about the dream, I wondered what the angry force was. Is there something I'm not dealing with that's stopping my progression? The next dream would show it.

I'm in a dark stormy rage. I feel like I'm going to kill anything that gets in my way! A black cloud is behind me as I descend a staircase.

Someone is on the staircase. My hands go straight for their throat in a death grip. Then I see the golden curls of my oldest daughter Sasha. She stares at me. It takes every bit of my power to remove my fingers. Strangling my daughter is not what I want to happen! I wake up.

Sasha was a creative child like myself. Was I trying to kill my child-self? As I looked out the kitchen window while washing the dishes, I felt something was indeed not right. In my mind's eye, I saw a little girl down in a pit. She'd been crying and wanted to get out, but couldn't do it by herself. I recognized her. She was little Mary, my childhood self. So I talked to her, "How'd you get down there?"

"You didn't love me and tossed me away."

How could I not love that cute little child? I probably blamed her for some poor choices I'd made. "I'm sorry. Let's get you out of there. You can ride on my shoulder and go everywhere with me. I'll try my best to always love you." I reached down and pulled her up, correcting the problem in my mind's eye and thus in my life.

I took another breath of realization. I didn't lose my child self as I grew older. She came along with me! So what was our childhood self? That was the part of our self that knew how to have fun, to laugh, dance and create. In my late sixties, I would write a book about that child self-called REMEMBERING ME. It's a story about my life from age three to four years old. I wanted to remember her and love all my "Me's" for life.

Chapter Eleven

If you are married, how do the two of you work out your finances? My husband Ralph was a compulsive bill payer. I complained to him about this problem. When he'd finished with the check book, there wasn't enough money to buy all the groceries I needed for the next two weeks. The next dream reminded me of our finances.

In the dream Ralph and I are walking down the street. I notice I have a large male lion strolling at my right side. I imagine a circus trainer must have given him to us, and told me the lion was hand raised. He walks along like a huge dog. We stop and he sits on the curb. I peer into his enormous pussycat face. He indeed seems gentle!

The lion lets out a little purr that means he's hungry. I say to Ralph, "We must find the lion some meat, maybe in that grocery store across the street". Then I think to myself about how hunger can turn gentle animals into raving beasts who will kill for their food! We hurry towards the store, while I keep a watchful eye on our pet lion for any signs of starvation.

The three of us enter the store. At the meat counter, I tell Ralph, "Get the lion something we can afford, like hamburgers or hot dogs". Ralph buys what I suggest, and we give the food to the lion. He starts to eat what is offered to him, but then he spies the sirloin roast. He jumps up on the counter, stepping into the case, and ravenously gulps it down. I'm embarrassed. I wish I didn't have a lion like this who walks all over the meat eating more than we can afford!

We manage to get the lion outside the store. I'm done with this lion. I'm leaving him to take care of himself, or to find someone else who wants him. I move away from the lion and into another house. I look back at the lion who is lazily sitting on the curb gazing around. I hope that he doesn't follow us.

After thinking about the dream, I knew I could manage the checkbook. I didn't have Ralph's anxiety. I talked Ralph into letting me handle the bills for the next month. All went well, except it made Ralph so nervous, he could hardly stand it. I felt sorry for his nerves and gave back the checkbook. I was always giving in to his pain or strong desires. I wanted him to be happy, but what about me?

I dream Ralph is insistent on showing me something. He has me by the hand and is pulling me along. I'm tugging back. I jokingly try to talk him out of the urgency of doing this now. It's not that I'm afraid, it's just not what I want to do. In order to make him stop, I would have to take a strong stand and confront him. It seems easier for me to be dragged along for now.

We seem to be out in the country struggling as we cross a tall grassy field. Up ahead, there's a rocky shore along a sprawling lake. I exclaim, "I've been here before!" I clearly recognize the shore and lake. Ralph takes me over to an old black car that is sitting on the beach. I'm still trying to talk my way out of this. He opens the back car door and pushes me into the back seat slamming the door behind me.

The car immediately flies up into the air in an erratic manner. It's like being on a wild carnival ride. I grip the open window and look down. I see Ralph watching me below. I call out, "What good is this going to do? I'm going to get myself killed!" I feel fear in the pit of my stomach as I steady myself by hanging onto the back of the front seat. I feel I must keep my wits about me and think fast. My survival is in jeopardy.

I awaken. I thought the moral to this dream was, "It's better to stand up for yourself in the face of all kinds of opposition, than run the risk of death." It looked like Ralph wanted me in the back seat! That was not where I wanted to ride in life. I needed to learn to say, "No", and stick up for myself. Maybe I was afraid it would be the end of our marriage. I knew I had a good brain. Where did I get the idea that men were in charge and women should follow their husbands? Ralph certainly believed in it.

I remembered in therapy group that Leonard had me yell, "No", a number of times. I guess I thought I should be a "Yes" person. It was ruining my life. I needed to take responsibility for what happened to me! Why did I think what Ralph wanted was more important than what I wanted? Where was the middle ground? Negotiate, negotiate!

When we married, I told Ralph right away that we weren't going to travel around the countryside living out of a panel truck as he wanted. Ralph had enthusiasm and energy. He was ready to leap in any direction his interests led him. But, you needed to think of the consequence before you leap. I guess my Pisces tended to throw water on his Aries fire sign. I did go along on the trip to Big Sur Hot Springs in the middle of the night, when we were first married. Kim Novak beat us there, so we had to wait until she left with her man friend. There, I had my first experience with nude bathing. When another naked man walked in and sat in our large square tub with us, I didn't know what to do. It didn't bother Ralph any, so I decided it was okay. I expected him to keep me safe.

Despite his faults, Ralph could be generous. I remember the time when I went shopping in North Bend. I decided to look at a ladies shop for clothes. I found a silky, cream colored blouse, trimmed in lace with matching three tiered full skirt. The next rack had a lovely, black satin, wrap-around blouse. I wanted them. They would look great on me, but I didn't think we had enough money for frills. As I went out the door, there was a pair of sandals that matched the dress perfectly, too.

At the dinner table that night, I described the beautiful clothes I had wanted. Ralph said to me, "Go back and buy them all for yourself." Permission can be a lovely thing. I didn't waste any time on acquiring the garments and sandals. (I still have those clothes in my attic, too many memories to let them go.)

I remember the time when Ralph wanted to take me out for dinner. His mother said she would baby sit our two daughters. Ralph ordered dinner with champagne. I knew it would take all our money, but Ralph was okay with it (the lion again.) We had a great time and I had a bit of trouble walking straight to the bathroom. I must say, I have never gone hungry or been without shelter. I guess everything works out, one way or another.

Chapter Twelve

Sometimes a dream tells me something about how life is for everyone. My family and I are staying in cabins at a wilderness retreat along with another group of people. My two daughters, Sasha five and Sonia age one, are staying in a cabin by themselves. I feel very sad at the thought of this. I want to be with them, but I can only visit them. I share a cabin with my husband Ralph. Our cabin is located about two blocks away.

We go to our children's cabin, and I'm putting Sonia to bed in her white crib. She's dressed in her pink fuzzy sleeper. She's so soft and warm to snuggle like a little rosebud sprinkled with dew. It's not Sasha's bedtime yet, so she is playing on the living room floor. I see her tangled blond curls and curious face. I'm saying goodbye to them. Ralph waits by the door. We must return to our own cabin. I know our girls will be alright, but I'm anxious and reluctant to leave them. Ralph reassures me they will be safe and we depart.

Back in our cabin, I can't go to our girls. Something is blocking my understanding of how to travel there. I feel an intense sadness on my heart! I worry for their care and protection. What if someone might try to harm them? They're so young. It's right that I'm with Ralph and yet, have I abandoned my children?

As I worked on writing my book, I knew the answer! All was as it should be. A gulf of time and stars separate our lives. I have my generation with my husband, while the girls belong to their generation. We must go our own ways, to visit only in love by the wings of a sea bird. I was blessed by this understanding.

My next insight came when Ralph had been home from work for a week with back trouble. He could hardly get around the house. Going to the chiropractor had only made him feel worse. No quick fix, just rest.

Before getting out of bed in the morning, I am aware that health and happiness are a matter of having my body tuned to its natural vibrations and rhythms. I needed to step out of my own way. As I laid in my bed, I felt a beautiful sense of health encompassing my whole body. I couldn't remember before feeling so healthy and wonderful. It was like a high, so gentle and peaceful. Then Ralph stirred beside me and I heard him suck in his breath in sharp pain. He was unable to change his position for the moment because of the ache in his lower back. I hoped he'd be able to realign his own self and throw off the burden of pain from mistakes. Pain will certainly stop you in your tracks so you have to think about what's going on in your life.

The next dream shows some of the struggles I was going through as I tried to make sense of my life and mistakes from the past I made along the way. I promised another past life dream, so here it is.

I dream of traveling with Ralph's sister Carolyn down a red brick hallway with no windows or doors. It doesn't seem to be leading anywhere, but then the tunnel ascends upward at the end. I say to Carolyn, "This is a transition period before we pass on to a different level."

It seems I am back in time at around the turn of the century. A large warehouse is being built by a big organization. They're trying to get people to rent the spaces for their businesses. I'm looking a room over with some other friends. The people who run this warehouse are gangsters and my friends and I have fallen under their power. We are running a shop as a front for some of their undercover activities, like booze, gambling and sex. One of my friends plays a pump organ to attract people off the street to hear some of the gangster's promotional ideas.

My boyfriend says we need to plan an escape to get out of the clutches of these people. He gets caught. I see, in my mind's eye, the gangsters holding him in an abandoned warehouse. They force another man to shoot him, on pain of his death. I'm broken-hearted about his killing. I decide I won't let the gangsters get away with this.

I sneak away and go to the police station. I tell the head detective about my boyfriend's murder, and show them pictures of some of the pornography they'd been pushing. The detective is rather distracted by the pictures, but I say even though he did something wrong, his death should not go unpunished.

I leave to catch the next ship out of the seaport. I'm aboard ship, but all the women are treating me like dirt, and don't want to be associated with me. I guess, because of my dealings with the underground vices. I feel awful, like the world has no room for me. My love is dead and everyone is closing me out, wishing me gone.

I get off the ship and look down into the green water between the dock and ship. I step back and watch myself giving up her life. She plunges into the water. Her body is straight and stiff, arms at her sides, teeth clenched. She wears a long white night gown. She falls like a stone into the bay, down, down into the depths of the ocean.

I find myself sitting on the stern of a half sunken, small wooden boat. I can see the sides of the railing sticking out of the water, outlining the boat's shape. A sailor has his arms around me and is comforting me. I'm sobbing so hard, I can't hold my head up. The sailor is going to take me home with him and love and comfort me, and I don't even know his name.

Because I was playing the part of the woman, I thought it was another past life of mine. A life that hadn't been productive and needed healing. I got to see what happens when you take your own life. The forgiveness of the heavenly father was there for her. She didn't know much about who she really was. So if you know someone who has taken their own life, they will be helped and loved from the other side, not punished.

In another life time, like the one I'm in now, I will have to make amends for those poor choices. It occurred to me that Ralph liked peek shows and wanted his own porno picture of me. Guess I was being confronted again with that kind of behavior. I've heard we come to Earth to work out past problems and to forgive what really never happened to ourselves in this lifetime. (Meaning, we made it up and played the part.)

I'm making changes in my present life. I've chosen a creative job for myself this time. I've worked for other people briefly, but always felt most challenged when doing my own art work, jewelry, writing and paintings. I've felt someone was painting the pictures with me, as though I was divinely guided to paint what I chose and loved. The pictures are alive. I want to share what I have learned. I appreciate myself and feel contented in my work. However, I will have to take a stand about Ralph's lust in our relationship.

I know I am guided to seek spiritual knowledge. It had everything I needed for happiness. If I would just stick up for me! In my later life, as I began to wake up to who I really was, I tried to use as much truth as I could to enjoy life. I realized by myself, I really knew nothing. I needed to be led by a higher source. I knew it was about sharing and love. I was a successful artist in my craft. I'd have to figure out the marketing side. Money doesn't equal success, but it's nice to have. So far, I haven't made much of it yet, but I'm certainly not poor. Life is an aquarium of creative ideas. God has given me everything. I should be proud of it and use my talent for the betterment of all.

Chapter Thirteen

As I continued in my marriage with Ralph, I had a startling dream about my high school class. I'm now at Pasco in our high school parking lot. The lot is full of chairs, all of different heights. I see the buses arrive and the students filing to their seats. In some of these seats sit my classmates. Our high school building is in the background. I pass by the seats and enter the high school. I somehow arrive on the second floor. It consists of just halls and windows. I walk through the empty halls. The windows line the hallways, so I can look out and see the students in the parking lot below. I stop where the stair would be, but there are no stairs. Instead there's a red brick spiral tunnel slanting rapidly downwards. It's hard to walk on, so I steady myself by putting my hands on the walls. I don't want to slip and fall.

Now, I'm on the same level as the other students. Across the street is a stage where our high school cheerleaders are doing cheers, while the students watch from their chairs. My destination takes me across the street and behind the cheerleaders. They do a jump where you kick one leg out and bend the other leg under. In jest, I copy the jump. My jump goes very high and I land perfectly. I'm pleased that my classmates see me do this. I too could be a cheer leader if I wanted.

I cross into a large mowed field, where some of our senior boys are practicing baseball. I stop near first base and look to second base where I see my classmate Richard standing. He throws the ball to first base to get the runner out. The ball hits the first base bag and bounces off, as the first baseman was gone chasing another ball.

I notice a small gold wedding ring on my left hand. I look over to see whose playing first base. It's Jim, a boy I had a big crush on in high school, but no one knew of this. I playfully tease him about missing the ball on first base. He jokes back. I sit down on the grass at short stop position, reclining on my elbows to watch the game. Jim comes over and sits in front of me, leaning his back against me affectionately. He begins to tell me how much he's always loved me.

I'm shocked. "Why didn't you tell me this years ago, things might have been different?" Jim turns and embraces me, kissing me in a deep passionate kiss. My blouse falls open revealing my breasts. Jim puts his mouth on my breasts, gently caressing them. I'm quite enjoying all of this, except we are in public! I feel uncomfortable about what others might think of us abandoning ourselves.

Jim hasn't notice my wedding ring. I show it to him. I say, "I've been married for quite some time, eleven years. All I can offer you is my friendship, and to meet my husband."

After journaling my dream, I was pretty amazed as I came out of my bedroom that morning. There were more marriage possibilities back in high school than I thought. But I was so shy about going up to talk to a guy who excited me. I'd just watch him from a distance.

I was actually surprised to have found that dream in my notebook, because I wrote my book much later. At that time Ralph and I had been divorced at least seven years. I was still single when I found Jim. I was a delegate to the Democratic State Convention in Tacoma. At the convention, I decided to see whether any of my classmates were delegates from Franklin County where I grew up. On the floor, I discovered delegate Jim. Pleasantly surprised, I started a conversation with him about what was happening in our lives. He said he was single, too. Jim asked me out for dinner after the convention closed. I was excited about the date. Here was my chance to find out what he was like. I remembered the dream I'd had of Jim at the baseball field long ago.

We had a romantic dinner on the waterfront and enjoyed talking to each other. When we returned to the convention center, Jim asked me up to his room. I'd been interested in finding out more about him, so I said, "Yes".

The kissing and foreplay were thrilling, but when it came to performance, Jim got intense and uptight. That stopped the fun for me, probably him, too. We managed to get through the act. I didn't want to linger, so said my goodbyes hoping no phone number exchanges would come up.

In my car on my way back home, I was relieved and glad that I hadn't gotten involved with Jim back in high school because I probably wouldn't have liked the sexual relationship. Some might not agree with me, but in life we sometimes have only one chance to make it good. I put Jim out of my mind.

Now, I'm 70 years old and married to my second husband, Raymond. I discovered on my class e-mails that Jim had died of cancer. Many of my classmates posted about their times with Jim. I mentioned my crush on him in high school, and how we had bumped into each other at the State Democratic Convention and had gone out to dinner together. Later, as e-mails were posted, I found out he was married and had surviving children. I felt a shot of guilt about what I posted, wondering if he'd been married at that time, but I just said dinner.

The week after Jim passed, I dream I am with my husband at one of our high school reunions. We are up on the second floor walking to our room, when whom should I see coming down the hall towards us, but Jim. He comes up to my husband, and asks if I could go with him. My husband Raymond steps aside and says, "Yes", this is alright with him.

I'm shocked! Past husband Ralph would not have liked this. I realize Jim has unfinished business with me even though he was deceased! I know what it is. Jim takes me to his room. He wants to redo the evening after the state convention, up in his room years ago! This time, as we slide into bed with each other, we are in a place of mutual relationship. I'm in a joking fun mood.

Jim says, "How do you like it?"

I quip back, "Upside down if you want." We begin making love.

I waken almost immediately after the dream. I thought, *Oh, my God, Jim must of carried our past sexual encounter with him all those years. He wanted to make up for his part in bed. He wanted me to know he was a good lover.* Forgiveness of the self was never too late, even after one has finished their earthy life! A month later I saw Jim's obituary posted on line. There was his wedding date. He lied to me about being single. Maybe he'd felt guilty when he tried to make love with me back all those years ago which caused the problem.

I told my husband, Raymond about that dream. I wanted to know if he really would have said "Yes". He confirmed he wouldn't have stood in the way of someone wanting to be with me. It was up to me.

I want to say here, Raymond and I have chosen an earthly relationship of faithfulness to each other. Dreams have no limits as to where they might lead, and anything can happen depending on the guidance or lessons to be learned. You are free in dreams to decide what you will do without history or earthly interference.

Chapter Fourteen

Back to my Fall City time. Sometimes what was going on in my life followed me into my dreams as in this next dream. Ralph and I are sitting in a booth in a crowded café bar. It's very noisy with people laughing and talking, and we seem to be in the center of it all. Then a bunch of young drunk adult males raid the place. They hassle and bump into people, roughing-up anyone who complains or protests about their behavior. After awhile the party crashers leave.

The dream continues the following night and we are in the same café bar and the exact thing happens again! I feel my patience is really being taxed. I turn to one of my friends and say, "It's because today is the 8th, an unlucky number." I decide I've had enough of this, and Ralph and I leave for home.

We are in our bedroom getting ready for bed, when I glance out the bedroom window. I see the whole crowd of people from the bar, including the roughhousers, coming toward our house. These people start sticking their heads into our windows and door, making a huge racket. I'm ready to fight for my peace and quiet! I begin shoving bodies out of my house and slamming doors and windows. One of the troublemakers has gotten into my living room. In the darkened room, we have a knife fight. We both manage to stab each other. It's a grab your gut pain, but not fatal!

The dream continues with Ralph and me out working in our vegetable garden. There's a piano sitting in the middle of our garden.

I walk over and sit down at the piano. I begin to play the Beatles' song "Yesterday". As I sing the words, my mood is of resolution. My voice is clear and on pitch and I don't miss a note.

When I awaken from this dream, I am pleased I hadn't hit any wrong notes. I hadn't even thought about whether I could play or sing the song. It just happened. The song was pointing to better days in the past, a sad song. Better days might have been before I married Ralph, since I ran into trouble right away with his erratic behavior. But for now, I focused on the two nights of drinking and being out late we'd just done. That kind of behavior needed to be stopped! I dreamed it twice because I wasn't getting the message about stopping. The unlucky number 8, probably came from the fact I'd been reading about numerology. I was also feeling my privacy was being invaded. I would fight against that.

Ralph decided to grow some marijuana in the back of our property in the swampy area. I protested, but he assured me no one would see it, and it would be a better product than what was on the black market.

When he harvested his huge bush, covered in blossoms, he hung it upside down in our shed. I was angry, because someone could walk into our shed and it would be discovered. When I was going to college, a lot of students got arrested for growing it. Ralph said, "It's only for a little bit while it dries out, then I'll hide it."

Most of our friends had smoked marijuana at one time or another. My first experience with it was down in Monterey, CA, where we lived after we married. I was pregnant and Ralph was working in a tavern on Cannery Road. Bob Dylan dropped it there, too! Ralph excitedly told me about it after work that day. Ralph pulled out of his pocket a couple of joints rolled up in white paper. He said they were grass. He could hardly wait to smoke it. Ralph was the smoker, I wasn't. I'd never heard of smoking grass before, and would have to learn how to inhale to participate. I didn't think it really made me feel much different. When I found out grass was marijuana, I was shocked. When I was in junior high school, the black people who lived on the other side of the tracks were frequently arrested for smoking it.

Back at the tree farm, Ralph carefully planned a pot smoking party. There were about six couples. It was after bedtime hours and our kids were in their beds, doors closed. After smoking, everyone flopped down and draped themselves all over the living room on their own little highs. I found it not very social, as they were not interacting, but tripping out. I found myself extremely relaxed and lay down on our bed. I hadn't realized I was so uptight.

After the party, I got intensely sick. I relieved myself and went to bed with my temperature all confused. I dream of seeing our old family doctor. He checks me over and tells me to go to his house to rest. His house is huge with expensive, modern furniture. I have my own room upstairs. I go to a dimly lit hall. When I look into my room, it's dark with no windows. I decide I couldn't get well there, but I needed to go to my mother's room. I picture her bedroom. It's large with a king size bed where I would have lots of room. One whole side of the room is glass. I'm standing at the window looking out on a lovely garden and pool. I go and climb into bed, sitting up against some fluffy pillows.

Then I hear knocking downstairs at the front door. I don't want to go down to the door. I know a group of teenage boys is down there looking for trouble. They think no one's at home. I know the door isn't locked, if they get in, they will wreck things and make a big mess! I go down the stairs and open the door. I say. "I want you all to leave right now! I live here and you have no right to be here." They smart off to me, but leave. I have trouble locking the door behind them.

This dream made me think I needed to go to a higher place in myself (mother's house) to get well again. The juvenile delinquent boys are my sickness or life hassles. Maybe, I was trying to do too much.

Later that week, Ralph's friend, who was an Internal Revenue Agent, called us. He was going to stop by for a visit. When we lived in Upper Preston, he and his wife had been our neighbors. The pot plant disappeared fast! No more marijuana parties. My ex-brother-in-law told me years later, he stopped smoking weed because it killed his ambitions. Now, as I write my book, marijuana is legal in the State of Washington, but I have no desire to smoke it.

As Sasha was getting to be a young teenager, she was more challenging and wanted her own way frequently. I saw my ego again in this dream. I'm angry with my oldest daughter Sasha because she did something I didn't like. I speak to her about this. She just smiles at me in a cool, "I'm not going to let anything you say matter." This attitude I see in her makes me feel more angry and helpless. I grab ahold of her shoulders and shake her. She remains her detached self. I want to hit her. At least, she would feel the pain of my presence. Instead, I release her and tell her to go to her room and stay there. She leaves, smiling happily to herself, gloating over her victory of being unmoved by me. I hear a voice say, "Enlightenment has to come from within."

I'm still angry with her as the dream continues. I'm leading a horse to find a pasture for it to graze. I tell Sasha to get up on my horse's back and sit still and be quiet! Pretty soon we come to a pasture of cows and horses. I need another horse for Sasha, as she is using my horse. I tell her to catch her own horse.

From the back of my horse, she ropes a furry, bright eyed colt, a pinto with white patches and reddish brown coat. She has roped it high up on the pony's front leg. This worries me, as I'm not sure if the horse is secured enough to not run away. I ask a person I see standing near us, if the rope is alright around the front leg? He answers, "Yes, it's fine." I check the rope again and decide the colt will follow us. But, I keep thinking, *isn't there a better place for the rope to be.* I look up at the head of the colt like the rope should be there.

As I woke and recorded my dream, I thought, oh, the problems of being a parent! I'd already learned about logical consequences from the book CHILDREN THE CHALLENGE by Rudolf Dreikurs, M.D., when Sasha was five years old. I could have used the book earlier if I'd known about it. A friend from Sasha's preschool recommended it to me. My ego would have me be mean and escalate the problem. Luckily, I thought better of it. Power struggles with my kids don't work, because they always win. They would go to extremes I wouldn't. It's time for me to give Sasha more room to take care of herself, though I'm not sure she can handle it. She hadn't secured the head of her horse. She'll have to make her own mistakes, as we all have done. Later in life, I learned to pick my battles carefully, of what's not going to fly, because I'd have to follow through and enforce it.

Chapter Fifteen

As I worked on my book, I became aware of a follow up book to THE COURSE IN MIRACLES had been written by Mari Perron, first receiver, called A COURSE OF LOVE. I started to read it. Jesus, the great teacher, was going to show us a way out of the Ego. I knew it would be challenging. I would have to keep reminding myself "Love is all that is real". I knew love was something to perceive in myself. What if I was continuous loving kindness flowing in union, the Universe forever and ever, right now?

I continued to work with my dreams: this one from Aug. 11, 1974, that pointed to a more enlightened way.

I dream of the deepest spot in the ocean, an ultramarine deep blue hole, probably caused by a meteor hitting the Earth millions of years ago. I'm with a group of divers who wish to explore the depths of the hole. We have a line running from our ship down into the hole. Our divers pass up and down the line, adjusting to the depths, and slowly surfacing as their tanks run out of air.

Suddenly, I know the hole was explored before by another civilization. I tell our crew. Those people dived down holding their breaths, but eventually were able to breathe under the water. I see them now at the bottom of the hole, breathing in water like it was air, while walking through a stone passageway. There must be a city there with treasures of great wealth! But, the first explorers didn't wish to bring these treasures to the surface with them. I get excited, because the treasures are still there. Maybe our divers will be able to bring the valuables up. Then I remember our divers hadn't been able to explore the deep hole yet, because their air tanks would run out.

As I pondered the dream, I thought perhaps the treasures were just to be enjoyed by those who could achieve its depths, and not something the rest of the world would understand but would corrupt and exploit it's real worth and beauty. The treasure signified changes in our society that were coming. There'd be those who'd be helped to reach the riches naturally, without drugs. They were going to share those gifts with the rest of us, to be immediately used in our own lives.

In another dream, I see that inspirations of knowledge appear as little gold Christmas bows floating through the air on white dishes. I'm awed by the gentleness of this.

It occurred to me that all inspiration comes from the inside out. I knew it was true of my artwork. My imagination found ideas and pictures floating around on the inside of me that I could use. *Can you grab one of these dishes for yourself to share with the world?*

As I continued to journal my dreams, I began to feel stronger and more certain of my path. I learned somethings in dreams that worked, though I could only control my behavior.

In the next dream, I'm in a small boat on a large blue lake. I'm fishing near some lily pads. I notice I don't seem to have any device for steering or rowing the boat, which concerns me. Still, I'm very busy working with my catch. I occasionally get out of my boat by standing on a red cellophane pad. It allows me to move across the top of the water to assist my fishing. I can sit on it too. Back in my boat I look up and notice I have drifted all the way across the huge lake to the other side. I worry a little about how I will get back but then continue my fishing on this side of the lake by a new group of lily pads. Friends arrive on shore to help me pull in the fish. They leave, and I begin to move around again on my red cellophane pad.

I thought fishing was a good sign and I've always liked going fishing with my parents. I didn't see the fish because, although they were there, they were under water. I was surprised about the red cellophane pad. It was like a boat in its self, and gave me an advantage with my fishing. Perhaps, the red cellophane symbolized my higher self-working with me to do the work I was sent to do. I was not in control of the boat. Crossing the lake would be, later in my life, where my friends would help me bring in the fish. I liked that thought! I would not be going back across the lake. These fish could be my artwork and books I'd written, or something I'm not even aware of yet. I needed to let myself be guided and not worry about where I was led (no way to steer the boat) somehow everything would work out.

The next dream shows my progress at coming out of my separate-self phobia. I dream I'm on an island with a few other people. We are supposed to be rescued. We do some maneuvers that bring us to the edge of the island. The ocean surrounds us with no other land in sight. Un-expectantly, branches drop down to us from the sky. I intuit I should fly out from under them. Two other people and I are able to do this. As we soar above the branches, my feelings accelerate. *I'm free!*

Feeling separated from others in my life was like being lost on a island without help. Together, we were one with no one left out, but we each have to be ready to fly freely.

Back home, I heard about an astrology class being taught in Redmond, a city about a twenty minute drive away. I decided to attend a class to find out more about my birth chart and how astrology worked. I learned about the twelve zodiac houses and the movements of the planets through each of those houses. As the planets move, they approach our natal planets. That is where the planets were at your birth. Their positions form aspects of those planets as they move around your chart; like a triangle, 120 degrees apart, or square, 40 degrees, sextile, 30 degrees, conjunct, right on, and opposition, straight across. I bought books to learn how to cast my husband's chart and other family member's. Some of my books were, THE HOUSES AND THEIR SIGNS AND PLANETS, a twelve volume series by Noel Tyl and THE PLANETS THEIR SIGNS AND ASPECTS. Astrology began to show up in my dreams.

I dream of a natal chart with planets placed around the circle, then the progression of the planets begin. I can feel the pull of the planets as they touch off other planets placed on the angles of my chart. These carry a much stronger influence, than when they touch planets not on angles. Next the chart shows my first house Saturn. There are some aspect of Saturn in my past life, showing no hostilities towards men. I should get along well with men.

I waken excited about that. I start thinking about my childhood. I preferred playing with boys rather than girls. They were not as fearful and would try more new things than girls would. When I was small my best friend was my cousin Jerry.

As I dream again I'm standing at the foot of an alpine green mountain. I see a man coming down a path off of this mountain. He greets me. He's warm and affectionate with black hair and beard; a rustic appearance. I say, "What have you been doing?"

He replies, "Teaching poetry to Pam."

Pam is my good friend. I'm surprised! I think poetry would be good for Pam. So I invite him to come home with me.

We are in my upstairs living room and Pam has joined us. I say to Pam, "You might as well tell him right off, you can't take him seriously unless he marries you. You need to propose to him and get that all taken care of first."

Then I turn to the man, "Have you ever had your natal chart done?"

"No." he says.

"We have had our natal charts done. My Sun is in Pisces, moon in Scorpio, and ascendant is in Gemini. Pam's a Sagittarius. You ought to see Pam's boyfriend's chart. They are exact opposites in personality. I could do your natal chart for you?"

He's interested and agrees to this proposal. I go get my astrology books I use for casting charts. He says he was born in a town in Germany. I stop for a moment, for I don't have the latitudes and longitudes for European cities, even though I know how to cast those charts. I say, "We'll need a map." He and I pour over a map in beautiful shades of blues and greens. I point to a spot on the map and say, "Is this the right place?"

"Yes," he answers.

I'm bending over a table to figure out the longitude, when he flirtatiously lifts up my skirt laying his hand on my bare ribcage. With his right middle finger, he thumps me as though he's a doctor. It causes me to feel pain like I might have appendicitis. I moan. He does it again and produces the same pain.

"Stop doing that! It hurts me."

He hugs me. "You've been eating too much food".

I'm amused. I've never heard that line before in order to get a hug. I smile. We both seem quite fond of each other.

On thinking of the dream, it occurred to me, I might be taking my Astrology and self, too seriously in daily life (eating too much.) I clearly realized that relationships are what life is all about. In dreams wherever my mind focused a relationship showed up.

I dream I meet Ralph. We are working on our present hassle in our relationship. I look down and see our feet are twisted and entangled.

The dream was straight forward. Our feet will carry us where we want to go in life. There were some differences about our directions in life, where we each wanted to go.

The dream changes, the girls and I are outside in a sheltered spot near an inlet of water. From a nearby island, a leafy branch stretches out over the water. On the branch sits a beautiful, iridescent blue bird. I'm overjoyed by the sight of this gorgeous bird! I point the bird out to Sonia, who wants to go over and touch it. The water is knee deep, so she wades carefully out toward the bird.

Un-expectantly, I see two people coming swiftly toward us walking side by side across the top of the water. It's a young man and woman, dressed in formal wear from the early frontier days. The man has on a top hat like Abraham Lincoln. The woman is wearing a longer, white dress with lots of fancy detail down the front and a flower wreath on her head. They stroll past us, their eyes looking into the future.

Thinking about this later, I knew the blue bird was about happiness. The couple dressed in clothing of the past suggested for achieving happiness, to look for values from past generations. Our present values have become corrupted. The man, like honest Abe, had good qualities for a relationship.

The dream changes. Ralph's younger brother Doug approaches Ralph and me. He is carrying a wrapped parachute. He says, "Mary, you are to make a jump from a plane that will fly high over this area."

Ralph says, "You'd better change your shoes and wear a pair of heavy duty boots for landing." I think my hiking boots would work. In my mind's eye, I see a flash of the map over which I would be dropping. There's a lot of water in this part of the country.

"I would also need a life jacket in case I land in the water away from shore. This would keep me alive until I can reach shore," I reply.

As I reflected back about the jump, it surprised me, how I wasn't afraid of the idea. Jumping out of a plane, would be one of my last choices, when awake, but then, so would divorce. I thought Doug might be trying to warn me of the end of my marriage, though I hadn't as yet been thinking about that.

Chapter Sixteen

I was fond of my brother-in-law Doug. He was a responsible, hardworking young man. He bought some land down the road from us, where he had also started growing trees. He had a lot of trouble getting along with Ralph. Their sun signs were squared, creating obstacles. One of our relationship therapy session involved wrestling another person. When I played with Ralph, he tried to overpower me. I found it to be no give and take. So I ask Doug if he would wrestle me. Doug was a great sport, and he was fun to wrestle. Later, Doug broke away from our family over a conflict with Ralph.

It happened when they bought a motorcycle together, probably Ralph's idea was to make it more affordable. Each time Ralph used the motorcycle he left it muddy. The two got into an argument about it. Doug decided he didn't want anything more to do with Ralph. I was sad, because now, our girls and I couldn't see him either, since Doug was afraid Ralph would be around. We had an un-relationship with Doug. I didn't understand much about forgiveness then, but I saw how Ralph's problems affected us all. The answer seemed easy to me, don't share a motorcycle together. They both took care of their stuff differently, of course it was more than the motorcycle and not the motorcycle. The Course says, "I'm never upset for the reasons I think".

I have a dream where I'm in a car driven by my husband. I'm in the back seat with some of his friends. We arrive at a hotel. On the third floor is a strip joint, frequented by prostitutes and their clients. Our group seems interested in going to observe what the atmosphere is like at the club. I'm not wearing anything from my waste up, so I think it's better not to go with them. I didn't want anyone thinking I'm one of the girls for sale.

Ralph and his friend go into the hotel. I fret on the sidewalk below, but curiosity has the better of me. I find a shawl to throw over my shoulders. I clutch it in the front, as I cautiously climb the stairs inside the hotel. I come down the hall toward the door leading into the night- club. There are two doors that open together, one is open and the other one closed. The top halves of these doors have windows. I see a prostitute standing across the hall from me. She gives me an odd look, as I peek through the closed door. A man is sitting on the floor inside, resting his back against this door. He turns, gets up and greets me warmly like an old friend. I don't recognize him.

He says, "Don't you remember me? You made me this beautiful shirt." He puts his hand on the collar to point it out. It's made of white Indian denim with pockets, cuffs and collar trimmed in blue print. I decide he must be one of Ralph's college friends. He comes out and gives me a big hug. He invites me to come inside to sit at his table with him. I seem to have all my clothes on now. I'm feeling better and appreciative of a friend's company. We go sit in a large booth in the corner of the room near the back door exit. Ralph and his friends see us, and they come over to join in. Ralph doesn't recognize my companion.

It's announced that one of the girls, who is famous for her dancing, will be performing next. Ralph says to me, "We're ready to leaving now." I don't think he likes me being with my new friend.

I reply, "I'm not ready to go just yet." They leave by the back door.

The announcer says everyone must bow and not look at the star performer as she inters and approaches the stage. Everyone in the room bows to the waist and looks at the floor. I make an attempt to do the same, while making a joke to my friend that this bowing is against my religion. I look up and see an Asian woman entering the room with her ladies in waiting. She is nude except for some white, see-through veils. When she reaches the stage, she is completely clothed and pregnant, wearing an Arabian outfit layered in veils. She has two small girls who are to dance around her. One girl slips off the stage and is helped back up. I don't understand this. My friend says, "The dancer will deliver her baby before anyone willing to pay to watch."

I find it distasteful that a woman would do this for money. I'm ready to leave now. I go out the same way I saw Ralph and his friends leave. But I can't find them anywhere inside the hotel. After a while, I finally make my way out of the hotel and back to the sidewalk where the car was parked. But it's not there! Ralph has left without me, and I don't even have my purse to make a phone call for someone to pick me up. I feel stranded and very upset that Ralph would leave me in such a helpless situation.

I walk down the street a couple of blocks and notice I'm now in a residential area full of large old, well built homes. I see a black woman across the street standing in her white wedding gown on the green grass next to the sidewalk. I think she looks beautiful.

Later, when I studied the dream, I decide the man I thought was one of Ralph's college friends, was probably my own guide, waiting to help me if needed. Interestingly, He'd said I'd made a shirt for him that sounded very spiritual in nature. I made clothes for Ralph, too. I hadn't been without a relationship in the dream, though Ralph seemed to have left me. The bride was a great symbol surrounded by well built homes from the past, which led me to think a marriage of a conventional nature could take place. The sidewalk was a good direction.

Two days later, after my alarm clock went off, I lay with my eyes closed, but my eyes were open on the inside. I'm viewing another beautiful world, not unlike our own Earth. The world seems complete in every way. I test it to make sure it wasn't an illusion. I walk up to objects and observe them closely. I pick up a rock to inspect it to see if all the fine cracks are in it, or if the flowers have veins in their leaves. Are the colors authentic and vibrant, the way I remembered them to be in the earthly world?

I walk along enjoying this land. I make mental notes like an explorer. There are some farms and a nearby town with wooden two story houses built right up next to each other as if they were connected like in Europe. I arrive at the edge of a field where I see a small passenger plane making an emergency landing. Its engines are on fire and the landing wheels are not down! As the plane descends, I look for a name on it, should it be a future disaster. The name is in a foreign language I don't recognize, maybe "Areox". Somehow, I think I could give warning, a head of time to the people who will die. The plane crashes to the ground and bursts into flames.

I knew without opening my eyes, that vision was a warning about a future family disaster.

Chapter Seventeen

At our nursery and tree farm our two daughters had Shetland ponies the neighbor found for them. I was happy we could give them that kind of experience. I always wanted a horse when I was a kid, but we lived in town when I was growing up. There was no place for a horse, so I would play I was a horse instead. On the playground, I talked a lot of kids into joining my herd.

Ralph's father and his new wife bought the property next to our nursery and tree farm. They lived on the back hill in a log cabin and had a roadside pasture. Their fields were where the ponies grazed to keep the grass down in the pasture. A young women asked Sasha's grandfather Bob if she could board her pregnant thoroughbred horse in the same pasture in exchange for the foal. Bob decided he was going to give the foal to Sasha as a gift. I was excited for her to have the opportunity to raise her own horse. Sasha's legs were almost dragging on the ground when she rode her Shetland pony named Goldie.

The thoroughbred mare gave birth to a filly Sasha named Domingo. She had her own horse, as my dream foretold. She trained the filly for riding. I gave her encouragement and any suggestions I thought might help. Sasha became easier to be around, as she was quite busy with her own mission to train and ride Domingo. There were some battles with Domingo, but Sasha managed to win. She became quite a good rider, racing her horse full speed, bareback around the town's logging track road.

The next dream shows Sasha and I are having fun together, probably because I didn't need to be finding something for Sasha to do anymore.

We are on a snow covered mountain side standing next to a huge, snow laden fir tree. The tips of the fir needles protruded out from under the layers of snow. The snow is so beautiful, heavily blanketing everything in sight. I'm in a happy sporting mood. We have skis on our feet. There's another woman here with us. I don't know who she is. The woman invites us to ski with her from the top of this huge tree to the bottom. The trail would spiral around and around the fir tree in a tight angle to the bottom, like a toboggan run.

Sasha's excited to go, but she's wants me to be with her. I agree to accompany her. We all stand in the air at the top of the tree. We line up and crouch down holding onto each other's waists. The woman leads, followed by Sasha, and I bring up the rear. Off we go! We travel so fast, I almost lose my breath. It's the most thrilling ride I've ever experienced! As we quickly arrive at the bottom of the tree and stop easily, we're totally invigorated from the tree ride!

It occurred to me that the women was showing us how much fun Sasha and my relationship could be. Skiing was not something our family had done yet, but it would happen in the future when Sasha was fourteen years old.

Dreams are so great because there are no limitations as to what might happen or what you can imagine. Nothing will be barred to express the lessons needed to be learned. Now if it's your fears, you're going to find out what they are. Unfortunately, this may be in all sorts of scary ways until you make a stand against the fear. Hopefully, if you do the right thing and don't run, you will find the answer and overcome your problem. If not, you will be revisited. Recurring dreams mean you haven't learned the lesson or dealt with the fear that your inner self is trying to teach you.

My friend Bob had that recurring dream problem. Because he knew I was journaling my dreams, he thought I might be able to help him. He told me of his nightmare. In his dream, he was being chased by two gigantic doughy balls, way bigger than he was. He feared he would die if they rolled over him! Since I knew Bob well, I had heard about some of his problems growing up. I knew what the fear was. He had a hernia when he was a kid and the doctors told his parents Bob could die without an operation. His parents were reluctant and put it off because of the cost. In the end, they finally consented to the operation which was a success.

Bob was being chased by his own balls! When I told him, he was so relieved and excited to know the problem. He could be done with the dream which haunted him for a life time. It was silly now to think his balls could kill him. In this world, a lot of problems are caused by unresolved childhood fears. Fears are never the real truth, but need light shown on them. That way, you can make a better choice to end the fear.

As I continued to learn more from dreams, I find myself in a clearing in the woods where barracks were built. I'm with a group of people, and we've been hired to repair these rundown buildings. I've been asked to go on a mission through the wilderness to the nearest town for supplies. I will be traveling alone. I set off on my journey with only the clothes on my back. I'm not afraid of being harmed or lost, because I sense the direction, like the needle of a compass always pointing north. I'm aware that a man from our camp who loves me, has a need to follow behind me to make sure of my safety. On returning from my journey to the barracks, I'm warmly embraced by this man. He tells me he followed 150 miles behind me the whole way.

I felt it was a loving act to be watched over in the dream but at that distance, how could he aid me if I were in immediate danger? I realized he could verify whether I survived or not. He was not to interfere with my trip but yes, watch over me. I trusted my inner-self which seemed to be doing well!

I feel more confident in the next dream. I'm on the third floor of a college building. I'm standing in a hallway, when I see a young women coming down the hall towards me. She has a spasmodic condition and holds her body rigid, in tight control in order to swing herself forward. I study her gait as she passes by me. I go over to her and say, "I think you could improve your walk by not trying so hard." I demonstrate my idea. "Let your body flow from side to side by using the momentum you have already started. Don't fight against it." She tries my idea and already her gait is much improved. At a quick glance, I wouldn't have notice her seeming disability.

That reminded me of how we try to cover up our perceived weak parts by over controlling ourselves, or not even trying. If I just let it go and let my true self function, then I could see what happens. It could be something great instead of the fear.

The dream changes and I find myself in front of some clothing racks of suede leather skirts and jackets in many dyed colors. I'm pleasantly impressed, because I know I can have any outfit I choose. I start sorting through the clothes, but I don't find what I want. I pass on this offer and move on down the street where I spy a small shop run by a black family. Inside their store is a showcase with merchandise on display. I approach the showcase and see three beautiful, wide belts, something I've always wanted. One belt is leather with laces up the front. The second one is woven in earth colors, and the third belt is embroidered in bright colors with figures on it. The third one is the most beautiful belt I've ever seen. I'm very excited and awed by it. I want this one!

In dreams, I noticed money was not usually an issue. We all were rich, unless we think we're not. I could choose, without a money limitation. Then what I choose becomes very important. I'd forgotten that in daily life, as I was so bound by thoughts of how much it would cost and could I afford it. The dream, I realized was not speaking to material things, but rather about what I might choose to symbolically wear through my journey in life. I loved my choice of the embroidered belt with people on it.

In my conscious life, I'd been frugal. Prices stopped me from buying things I didn't think I could afford. The budget came first, leaving clothing and entertainment for last. To save money, I sewed and knit my children's and my clothes, and even some of my husband's outfits. Mother taught me how to sew, as it was more of a must in her day, with manufactured clothes available mainly in the bigger cities. Ralph bought most of his clothes at Goodwill, as a holdover from his poor college days. To bring him into style comparable with the Beatles, I made him some bright colored suits. Sewing costs as much as cheap clothes, but I ended up with a nicer, more expensive looking outfit. You can also pay a lot of money for fabric, if you want. In the end, I was proud of what I made. There was time for sewing, because I wasn't holding down a conventional job. I worked for myself and the family.

Sometimes we seemed well off, as shown in this next dream. Our family is living on the ground floor of a hotel we own. It sits in the middle of a large green lawn. Ralph decides to mow the lawn. Between our property and the next one is a strip of dry grass and some pine trees. Ralph decides it would be good to take care of this strip too, even though it doesn't belong to us.

I'm outside with him. I feeling happy and my body feels very light. The sun is shining warmly, so I decide to see if I can fly. I stretch my arms out wide and start to run. My body lifts off the ground and I'm flying like a glider. My intention is what makes me fly. With the tip of my arms I can go in whatever direction I want.

Ralph turns and sees me up in the air. He excitedly runs to get a camera, because he wants some proof of what I'm doing. As I fly, I know he should not take a picture! As he gets ready to click the shutter, I suddenly lose altitude and fall flat on my belly in the grass before he has time to take the picture. Ralph leaves and I go back to my flying practice.

I'm now about thirty feet above the ground. As I hold my position in the air, I'm very tuned into the air currents and can feel every little change of direction in the flow. I try to see how swimming strokes will work. I try the scissor kick and it moves me forward. Next, I do the crawl and the breast stroke. I decide they are not very suited for flying, even though the strokes will move me forward. They jeopardize my ability to float, because of all the effort it takes to do them. My intention to fly, gliding and using the air currents work best. I land and go into our hotel to our apartment.

It turned out in wakeful living that some of the dream came true. Ralph decided to put in a long lawn between our property and the road easement that rans toward Snoqualmie Falls. He kept it like a golf course. He installed a wooden, hand craved sign on the grass that said, "Raging River Nursery." I often heard him grumble if someone threw cans or garbage on the lawn while driving by. He'd be back out there picking it up.

Perhaps my flying in the dream was showing me my progress on dream work, becoming lighter and happier. Ralph needed proof of my flying, which I felt was wrong. It was all about inner trust.

Sometimes my dream-self showed me a more productive way of working with a group of people. Here is the way it started.

Ralph and I are part of a singing troupe. We are dressed in our formal wear for a sing-out. Our troupe is walking to the place of our performance that goes through a residential community. I have gone ahead. I cross a green, park looking boulevard to the other side of the street. I continue up the sidewalk past houses, when a man jumps out from behind a large tree and grabs me! Trying to hold me steady with one arm, he frantically scoops a handful of Grape Nuts off the ground and tries to force his fistful of Grape Nuts into my mouth. The Grape Nuts fall all over me and the dirt, because I refuse to open my mouth. I'm very startled by this violence to my person. I'm also relieved it isn't a sexual assault! He bends down to grab another handful of Grape Nuts, but I decide I've had enough of this! I holler out for Ralph who I know is in hearing distance. Ralph comes running. Seeing a large, stronger man coming toward us, my attacker quickly lets go of me and flees.

In my marriage with Ralph I felt safe from another's harm, because Ralph was a big strong man and would protect me. I used Ralph's size to intimidate my assailant. I actually liked Grape Nuts but not being suddenly forced to eat them from the ground by a stranger!

Back with the singing troupe, we continue to the place of our concert and perform our program. As our troupe walks back home, we see another singing group walking in the same direction but on the other side of the street. They look over at us and make gestures and hostile faces. They gather together in conversation about us.

I'm concerned about the rising trouble. Just because we are part of the same competition and in the same business, is no reason to be enemies. Instead, this is more reason to be friends. We share a lot in common in our experiences as singing professionals and the type of personalities that choose this work.

I call out to the other troupe, "Come across the street and walk with us in friendship." They decide to take my offer and fell into line with us, happily chatting with our members as we all continue on our way down the sidewalk.

On awaking, I was very pleased to have seen the peaceful solution in the dream. It could have gotten ugly. I will have to remember to use that way to dispel unpleasant competitions. Let's talk together and share ideas.

Chapter Eighteen

Sometimes when I dream, I've encountered well known or famous people. There is usually some insights I needed, something they represented to me that needed to be learned.

In this dream Ralph and I are at what looks like a modest version of the White House where the President of the United States, accompanied by his wife are going to speak. As they walk into the room I'm startled to see they are just like one of us watching, friendly, homey, and middle class in appearance. I recognize Gerald Ford and First Lady Betty Ford. They both speak to us about a subject unrelated to politics. When the President and wife leave, I walk them to their Presidential limousine. The car is a beautiful shade of dark blue, elegant and regal looking. Its design reminded me of an old model of a Rolls Royce. If you saw it drive by, you'd turn and look to see who was inside.

Gerald Ford gets into the driver's seat and First Lady Betty Ford takes the passenger's side next to him. I'm surprised to see her seat is a small cuddly bed, complete with pillow. She snuggles down comfortably to sleep. I say to her, "That is a very unusual idea."

She says, "I like it this way because I can sleep while Gerald drives." The limousine is now moving down the street and remarkably, I'm inside driving it. I see a man lying in the road blocking our way. I know this man is trying to get the President's attention by making us stop and listen to his concerns. I pretend to turn left and the man jumps up running to block our way again with his body. At the last second, I quickly turn right before he can stop our passage.

We arrive at a park and slowly drive across the grass towards the children's swings and playground equipment. There's a group of young adults standing in this area. I know we won't be able to pass them without stopping, because they will recognize the limousine and know of our significance.

As I thought about this dream, I had several insights about myself and my attitudes. I found it refreshing that the President and First Lady are regular people. However, I also thought the First Lady should take a more active role at the White House. As in the future, President Obama's First Lady Michelle Obama would do. Though the President could avoid power plays, he would need to be aware of the younger generation's needs and wishes.

As I go through life, I assumed some of society's concerns and fears, like were there flying saucers, UFO'S. Had spaceships landed on our planet? Would they try to attack us or be friendly? Here was one of my dreams demonstrating such fears.

I'm in a small, sprawling town standing next to an army barracks. I look up into a clear blue sky. Suddenly, I see a fleet of large black spaceships, not like any airplane I've ever seen. They must be from outer space! As they come closer they look like huge buckets capable of transporting thousands of people. When they touch down, I notice wide flat fold-up ramps descending from their sides. I know the spacemen have come to harvest our people and take them back to their planet to eat! Earth is just a big stockyard to them.

I run to the barracks where Ralph, Bob, his girlfriend Margaret and another couple are staying. I tell them, "We are being invaded!" They all dash to the windows to look out. We watch some of the spacemen hunting our people. They look just like us except their faces, bodies and clothes are all the same. They all have the same intent and purpose of capturing everyone. They go quickly and thoroughly about their work without causing much pressure or violence, because all they have to do is lock eyes with their victims, then the person becomes mesmerized and will follow them anywhere.

I weigh the situation: we could give ourselves up and be herded aboard to be taken back to be devoured like everyone else. There might be some comfort in accepting the same fate as the others and not fight it. Or, we could see if we can escape and hide until they had gone. Maybe we could survive on our own. I turn to my husband and say, "It was good we at least had our last night together."

Quickly a spaceman comes into our room and walks up to the other couple, mesmerizing the wife. We all flash a glance at each other and all at once decide to fight! We all jump on the spaceman and we drag him to the floor and tie him up. Two other spacemen have followed him. We grab them too, doing the same thing to them. Ralph decides that Bob, the other man and himself will strip the spacemen of their clothes. Their plan is to impersonate the spacemen and lead us toward the spaceships, then we escape.

Outside we see a number of buildings being set on fire to smoke out our people. We hurry through the town. None of the other spacemen questions us, all are too busy with their own work of capturing people. Eventually we make it out of town and climb a big hill where there is a plateau overlooking the town. I'm feeling relived and relatively safe. We walk away on a road through the countryside. Along this road, we find signs posted saying *500 people lost here to spacecraft, 32 people lost,* and so on down this road, giving us the death count.

I was startled by the dream. "Oh my God, I hope that doesn't happen." Our friends had made a strong threesome in the dream. Bob had already separated from his wife and had brought his new lady Margaret into our circle. Margret was straight laced English, except for being an Aquarian. She had two children, Mark and Adrian from her previous marriage. They were close to our children's ages. I liked her. Life was tough being a single Mom. The father was not around. It worked out well when our friends had children, because the kids would go off and play together leaving the adults to visit and share experiences. Everyone was age appropriate. We all had problems to deal with when raising children. My next dream showed this.

I'm out on a low hill with sparsely scattered pine trees. The ground is very dry, covered with short, brown grass. Ralph owns this area and has marked it off into sections for me to weed. I have my shuffle hoe in hand and I'm systematically removing weeds. As I quietly work away at my job, it occurs to me Ralph has given me way more work than I can possibly get done without help. I worry about what I can do about this. I tell myself, *well, I'll be able to complete this section."* I smile, *he'll have to help me with the rest of it if he wants it done.* Then I hear a piercing scream. It's my daughter Sasha's voice! From the sound of her cry she is some distance away. I run down the hill to the road and look down it toward where I heard the sounds of her voice. I hear her screams again and also the growls and snarls of a wild animal! I'm very anxious to know what is happening, but I can't see all the way down the road because a dust like fog is obscuring the view. For some reason, I know I must not go toward her. She must come to me. I'm very distraught and nervous, hoping she will be alright until she reaches me.

I begin to see her shape coming through the fog running as fast as she can. She's terrified as a big black wild dog is chasing her snapping his jaws at her ankles while growling ferociously. I call out, "Hurry, hurry, Sasha! I'm over here." She reaches me panting breathlessly and jumps behind me. I have my shuffle hoe in my hands and jab it at the wild beast, forcing him back. His continuous growls ring in my ears as he dodges my swings and pokes. I can't seem to connect with his body to give him a solid blow. I keep swinging even though we are losing ground. The dog hasn't been able to get at us either. I'm determined to wound this attacker and put an end to the threat on our lives. Finally, after a quarter of a mile of fighting, the dog begins to give up. He looks doubtfully at me and moves off eyeing me sideways. I'm so intent on trying to wound him, I can't seem to stop. Besides, he could circle around and come back at us. I lunge at him giving him a slicing blow on his side. I have wounded him! He yips and crumples into a ball. I feel strong and victorious! I have taught him a lesson!

I look down at the heap of dog. He has transformed into a tear faced little eight year old boy who is holding onto a metal pipe, the kind you would hang clothes on in a department store. He is bleeding on his side under his arm. At the sight of this, I feel terrible for having hurt what turned out to be a sad child. What will people think of me and how will I explain myself? What an empty victory this turned out to be. I'd better take a look at his wound to see if he's alright and perhaps get some help for him.

I pondered this dream. Who or what was threatening Sasha. I thought of my husband, Ralph. I had defended Sasha a lot against her father's critical judgements. I knew his childhood had been very difficult. His own father had been so critical and strict with Ralph, the first born and also with his brother and sisters. I don't think I heard any happy tales of his growing up. I know Ralph's father had regrets at the end of his life.

I had to defeat the mad dog to learn that behind the attacker was a hurt child, not to be destroyed, but to be helped in stopping his painful behavior. He needed love. I knew Ralph had problems when I married him and I thought loving him would clear it up, but I can't make Ralph love himself. I will protect my children. In THE COURSE IN MIRACLES it said, either we are giving love or making a plea for it.

Chapter Nineteen

Sometimes I had dreams that told me about the arrival of persons to visit us.

I'm in my house in this dream, (which never really looks the same in dreams except that it's mine). My house is constructed in the middle of a four way crossroad, part of it is outside and part is inside. I go outside and walk down my west road and up a small hill. I call out, "Is anyone out there who wants to come in?" A figure appears on the road a distance ahead of me, then advances rapidly screeching to a halt in front of me, big as life! I'm quite startled, but recognize my brother-in-law Gary who's in his mid-twenties. I say nothing and turn and walk back to my house.

Inside, I hear a knocking at my door. When I open it, there is my older sister Linda, her husband Gary and a bunch of their boisterous friends. I invite them in, thinking to myself, *Gary really did want to come visit me.* Their group wants me to go to a night club and theater with them. We listen to a blond singer at the night club. At the theater I see an actress take a costume out of a trunk. I ask her, "Why did you choose that costume for your performance?"

The dream foretold the arrival of my sister Linda, Gary and their two daughters, Shawn and Shelly. They have come for a visit at Fall City. Sasha and Sonia were very happy to have their two cousins come to play. They all had wonderful fun, because our neighbor had found a pony cart for our girls that Sasha's Shetland pony could pull.

With all of them piled aboard they took turns driving it over the nursery paths.

Linda, who had started dying her hair blond in high school and also liked to sing, married Gary when she was fifteen years old. I cried at her wedding, not out of happiness.

What brought on the early marriage was: Linda and I were at the movie theater watching a Disney movie. Gary shows up and she leaves with him for a joy ride. By the time I sat through most of the movie a second time, Mother crept down the aisle looking for us, no Linda.

Gary brought Linda home the next morning. She had begged him not to take her home for fear of punishment, but what could he do? He was now in trouble, too.

Gary was the oldest of eight children and his parents were alcoholics. After watching his parents when growing up, Gary never touched alcohol. He was very popular in high school with his ability to talk to everyone and later, became a successful salesman. My sister ran with the popular crowd too. Everyone thought they married because of pregnancy, but it wasn't true. I was friends with Gary. We both were Pisces, born one day apart, only he was two years older. I call him a friend to this day.

We took our families up to Snoqualmie Falls, a local attraction in our area. I couldn't believe it when Gary climbed the cyclone fence and crept over to the wet edge to look down! I turned to my sister in protest, but she just shrugged it off. I thought to myself, I wouldn't want to be married to someone who did dumb things like that. Though, Ralph was just as crazy in his own way, like climbing a telephone pole when he was drunk.

At our house, Ralph thought he could see through Gary. He baited him and afterwards would feel like a top dog when Gary got upset. Ego plays are never nice and can break relationships. Linda was pissed at Ralph. I was mostly at a loss for what to do. Family members should try to get along. We can't control others. Forgiveness can free us to fly again, but we might want to be more cautious with whom we visit.

I found another dream where I saw a large, circular horoscope chart on which both Ralph and my planets move together. I point out to Ralph where my planets are and how I feel about it. Ralph shows me some of his planets but is reluctant or unwilling to tell me where all his are. He only reveals partial information concerning how he feels about their placement.

As I pondered the dream, I thought Ralph was concealing something from me and not being truthful, perhaps about our future together.

I found another dream that addressed this subject. In my dream, I'm to meet with Ralph and a teacher, where the topic of discussion is going to be one of my past dreams involving Ralph and me. The teacher is discussing the dream for us to increase our knowledge of ourselves in our relationship. The teacher feels my dream is very important. We all enter into a lively discussion of the dream's meanings, our positions of self and why. During the discussion, I sometimes feel enlightened, a little self-conscious and full of questions.

As I begin to awaken in the morning, I hear myself saying a silent prayer to God to grant me the strength and guidance to accomplish what I must do in my lifetime. I can't remember which dream of mine was discussed or any more details than what I've told you. I thought it was because I wasn't to be too consciously aware of it. Other times I thought I couldn't because it scared me and the knowledge wanted to flee my consciousness.

Chapter Twenty

We are constantly being bombarded throughout our lives with choices. Many of these choices also have symbolic meaning as we travel on our paths.

I dream I'm in a collectors' shop on the second floor of a large brick building. The shop is full of art objects from past to present. Some are very rare and unique, centuries old, things I haven't seen before like a metal woven bib collar. The furnishings of the shop are very plain, rough planked floors, white plastered walls with simple wood trim. There are two glass counter showcases a cupboard and a bureau with some paintings on the wall. There is another adjoining room. Everything is for sale, not just display. The sales clerk sits behind the showcase next to the bureau. I go over to a chest of drawers. On the top ornate drawer handle is hooked a plain brass bracelet. I ask the clerk, "Why is this bracelet hooked over the handle?"

He says, "I don't know. I couldn't get it off."

I twist the bracelet around until it slides off the handle. The clerk is surprised. I say, "If it will go on, it will come off. Can I have the bracelet?'

The clerk answers, "Yes."

My youngest daughter Sonia appears by my side. I bend the brass bracelet to fit her small wrist and slip it on her. As she examines it, the bracelet becomes covered in small white stones that sparkle like diamonds. Sonia is overjoyed with it. I think to myself, *I hope it doesn't turn out to be cheap rhinestones.*

Ralph and I walk into the second room, where I find some purple glass containers sitting on the floor under a shelf. I say to Ralph, "Let's buy one of these containers. I would like to admire it. I'll find something to put in it."

Ralph answers, "Where would you put it? It's so large."

I look again at the container. I'm startled by a huge, purple cylinder, as tall as a person, now extending through the overhead shelf. I stop to think about these changes. The rest of the purple containers are all different in some way, either by shape or lid design. As I glance down the shop dog appears. He resembles something out of Dr. Seuss. He's a long wiener dog with a lumpy body on short legs. His neck is long and he has a pointed nose and floppy long ears. I'm afraid he might bump into objects as he snakes along from side to side, but he seems quite aware of where his body is walking.

We turn around and go back into the first room. I discover a new piece has arrived in the shop. A wall hanging, gorgeously painted on a free form piece of metal in brilliant colors. It's a portrait of a long haired man with beard from the bible period, maybe Jesus or a disciple. Hanging down from the portrait, running horizontally at top and bottom, is a royal blue drape with glittering sparkles throughout the fabric. The drape hangs at different levels creating an artistic affect. I think the piece must have come from a church. I would love to own it, however, it would look out of place in my modest home. Someone with lots of money would probably purchase it. They would have an elegant place to display it.

As I ponder my life connection to this dream, I think about my daughter Sonia. While she was growing up, she loved classical gold and diamond jewelry. She was not as fond of my handcrafted jewelry made from brass, silver and copper, and whatever I could find in stones, shells, beads and fossils. From simple brass can come something of great value. I continue to admire the color purple and wear in often. As a child, some of my favorite books were by Dr. Seuss with his funny animals and people that were so original and are collector's items now. I was searching for spiritual meaning and wanted it in my life, as was symbolized by the portrait. The portrait illustrated my spiritual longing rather than a physical object desired for my home. I now follow the teaching of Jesus, dictated through a medium in the COURSE IN MIRACLES and LESSONS OF LOVE.

Dreaming again, I meet a teenage girl. She tells me she can't find her mother. The young woman lives near my family's home, so I say to her, "I'll help you look for her." When we arrive near our homes, it's winter and very cold with two inches of snow on the ground. I look around and see little shacks built from whatever the poor people living in this area could scavenge. They have no fuel to heat their shacks. Nearby is our little chicken yard with a few chickens walking around inside. As we passed by, I check them to see if they are alright. Down at the edge of the snowy field, we come to my friend's house. It's a small, old farm house her family had found. We open her front door to a cold, empty house. Her family must have moved out, leaving her behind.

I study the ground around her house and discover her mother's tracks in the snow. As we follow the tracks, we find blood on the trail. A short distance ahead is a tiny shed, consisting mainly of a door. I open the door, and there by the edge of the door jamb is our Rhode Island red rooster squeezed in tight behind a board. Her mother was starving and stealing our chickens. She came to the shed to eat them. Apparently, our rooster was going to be next. The crumpled rooster pulls himself out and flies through the door, across the snow and lands in the shallow water of the icy creek. I think to myself, *that rooster is really dumb for he's not a duck. He'll freeze himself to death in the water.*

My adopted friend and I walk back to my family's chicken yard, where we find Ralph working on the chicken shed to make it more weather tight. I tell him, "My friend is going to stay with us for a while." Ralph begins to make room for her by laying a tarp down outside on the snow and placing our children's sleeping bags on top of it where he was planning for them to sleep. *This was not what I had in mind!* I object, "That won't be warm enough or safe for our girls to sleep out here in the open at night."

Ralph disagrees. "They'll be quite alright. You're overly concerned."

"Can't we all just share what little room we have together for a while?"

On waking, I'm shocked that Ralph would put our girls outside to make room for another young women. I was just trying to help her, not disarrange our family. Guess, I'd better watch out who comes home with us. Stealing our chicken wasn't a good development. This could be envy, because of a deficiency in the mother, not knowing where their higher selves were. The background surroundings weren't displaying a wealthy area of the self either, followed by a rooster who had no good sense, and was about to be had, which sounded like my husband. Guess, I was dumb to the motivations here, until I studied the dream.

The young woman, who shall we say, broke the camel's back was ten years younger than me. Her name was Ruth. She was married and lived in an A-frame house built with her awarded insurance money from her father's death in an airplane crash. I was amazed at being challenged by a younger woman, when I was only thirty years old. I thought that mainly happened to older women. She took advantage of our friendship and Ralph didn't need much encouraging. While I'm on the subject, good looks won't save you either, so look for the faithful, loving heart.

When I had gotten over being angry with Ruth and Ralph, I realized she'd done me a favor by bring to an end the tailspin of infidelities that just weren't going to stop while I was married to Ralph. I was left with wishing I'd never married him in the first place. My parents advised against it, but who listens to their parents at that time in life. The marriage was a part of my life, not all bad, and I had two lovely daughters to show for it.

My next dream has Ralph serving time in a penitentiary, from which he is going to be released as soon as his clothing is repaired and presentable. I go to a nearby store and purchase the items to repair Ralph's work shirt. The cuffs are worn and there's a rip in the elbow. A guard at the prison pays for my purchases since they are required for his release.

When Ralph is released, he, two other officials and I go out to dinner at a restaurant. There are many empty round tables covered with white cloth. Our party has the place to ourselves. We eat and enjoy our time together. After dinner, I notice this big restaurant has a landscaped, kidney shaped pool outback.

In the pool children and alligators are playing! I'm told the alligators are very gentle, so they won't harm the children. Startlingly, a large alligator roars up out of the water, showing his sharp teeth and lashing the surface with his tail. I'm concerned about the children. The alligator looks angry, not gentle, though he hasn't attacked anyone yet.

Studying this dream, it looked like I was still trying to help my husband and continue our marriage, regardless of the problems. Taking care of others all the time was a way to avoid myself, but was it accomplishing anything?

Here is a dream about my high school self. I'm attending my old high school, except the building is constructed differently. There are two stories, but inside the classrooms are enclosed only on three sides. The side where the door would be opens onto a narrow hall running by all the rooms. My class is on the ground floor. I'm dressed nicely with my long hair neatly arranged on top of my head. I am feeling very conspicuous like a new girl in a strange school. I do recognize a few of my old classmates' faces, but I didn't usually speak to them on a personal basis. I feel isolated and not part of the group, a beautiful misfit. I sense some hostility from some of the guys because of this.

The male teacher calls all the girls to come sit around his desk. We will be working together to solve some problems, while he works with the boys. I feel much better being one of the group of girls working together.

After class, I go out to my car in the school parking lot. I'm going somewhere, maybe home. I'm met by four young Italian men, strangers. They hurry over to me as I get into my car. They're stumbling over each other trying to be of service to me and get me to notice them. They ask me if they can start my car or drive me somewhere. I'm nervous and afraid they want to entice me away and rape me. I politely refuse all their offers and climb into my car closing the door behind me. The men begin to move off as I roll up my window and quickly push down the driver's side lock.

When the guys see me lock the door, they become quite angry and run around my car to the passenger's side. I scramble across the front seat just in time to lock that door, too. Then I notice the small visor window is open. I try to get this closed before they see it, but to no avail. One of the men forces it back tearing off of a piece of chrome, while the other men beat on my car. As he reaches his hand inside to unlock the door, I try to stop him, but he is too strong. I jump into the back seat. A mean angry face glares at me over the front seat. The man grabs me by my wrists and drags me out of the car.

All of a sudden, we all become aware of a cool eyed, blond haired woman standing on the school steps observing the whole scene. The guys quickly let go of me and run off. I walk straight over to her, very scared and shaken-up and feeling lucky to have gotten away because of her presence. I recognize her as a student from my class. Her name is Bonnie. She's a straight A student and social climber with the intellectual group. I pour out my story of what just happened. She's very sympathetic and understanding. She says, "This is my special work to handle cases like yours."

I reply, "I guess I should go to the school office and report this incident." She nods and accompanies me to the office. At the office I say, "I want to write down what happened." Bonnie goes behind the counter to get something for me to write on, but instead brings out some plaques you would use to engrave for a special deed, championship or honor. I'm confused. You don't give a medal for having a terrible experience like mine! She compares two or three of the plaques to see which she thinks is the best for me. Then the student counselor walks in the door. I turn to him with my story. He patiently listens to my troubles, then smiles and points to Bonnie. "She handles problems like this."

I go back to class, this time on the second floor. The students are taking their seats. I don't know what subject is being taught in this class, so I look at the cover of one of the student's book that lies on his desk. THIS IS MY HISTORY CLASS. I don't have any books with me, so I decide to go to my locker and get my books. I'm worried the bell will ring before I'm back making me late for class, but at least I'll have my text books.

I hurry down to ground floor and find my locker on the back of a student's chair that faces the hall. The class is in session, so I kneel down to work the combination. I find the first two numbers which are both 32, but I can't recall the last number to retrieve my books. This is the way it seems, I only know half of what I'm doing.

Thinking about this dream, I remember I did have trouble fitting in at school. Conformity was not my thing. I usually had one or two good friends and the rest were acquaintances. I had leadership ideas, but was not good at getting a following. I had a mistrust of men and their motives. I did figure that sex was the main game to be avoided while in high school. Paranoia caused fear where no danger really existed. I know if I expected the good from people, they will most often give it to me. The reverse is also true. If I can stay out of fear, I'm safe. So I'll accept my gift plaque. I had survived.

Part 2

Chapter Twenty-One

My premise, we live our lives from the inside out, still surprised me. Recently I came on a dream from my journal that showed this way in advance of it materializing in my life. At the time, I was faithfully writing them down, looking for my spiritual self, not looking back and certainly, not thinking about whether it would happen in the future.

As my dream begins, I have agreed to a date with Ron for sexual intercourse. The place of our rendezvous is his attic. He is married to Sherry, who is the ex-wife of Pam's man friend. (Not true in real life.) We are in the attic on a double bed screwing. I'm on the top position. I have a flash through my mind I'm breaking my agreement with my husband by doing this: a guilty thought. Ron says, "I can't climax by sexual intercourse. I have to get my armpits rubbed hard to orgasm." I do this for him and he has a noisy climax. As we are getting up, we hear Ron's two teenaged boys coming up the stairs. I don't want Ron to leave because I haven't been satisfied yet. I suggest we move into an adjacent attic room for more privacy and shut the door. Ron is reluctant, being rather discouraged with sexual intercourse. There's a double mattress on the floor. I embrace him saying, "Just pretend you're a good lover and having a great time." I glance around once more and notice the walls between these two rooms are very flimsy, and his boys are trying to peek in. I toss my coat over one crack, but it hardly helps. The wall is useless.

I give up and we go down stairs. His wife Sherry is in their basement living room and she is very angry at us. She pouts and folds her arms across her chest as we walk by headed for the door. In the living room by the front door, I see three baby carriages full of clothes Ron has ordered to please me. I tell him, "Please return the carriages of clothes, because I won't be needing them." I say goodbye and close the door.

Out on his front doorstep, my friend Pam is waiting for me. She smiles and asks me how it was, assuming I had a delicious time. I answer, "No, it wasn't successful. I had to give him something like a blow job for him to climax by rubbing his armpits!"

The dream, though acted out in sexual form, was really telling me how our relationship would go, not about our sexual side. I did have an affair with Ron after Ralph announced he wanted a divorced. Because the dream came in advance of that action, I felt the moment of guilt. Ron was in his third marriage at the time, thus the angry wife who found out. No thanks to my jealous, soon to be ex-husband Ralph, who snooped into my notes and found my meeting date with Ron at a restaurant. Ralph then, tipped off his wife.

Ron's sexual problems in the dream were because he got bored with the domestic side of his relationships. In this case, Ron liked to fantasize about sex with teenage girls: the armpits in his case. He was eight years older than I. I had always been mistaken for looking younger than I was, even to this day. So I guess I qualified for the teenage role with the noisy climax. The three baby carriage of clothes would not keep me in the relationship. I eventually left. Pam waiting on the front door step, came into the dream because she'd told Ron that Ralph and I were splitting up. At the time, Ron was thinking of separating from his third wife. So he made a visit to me at my studio to see if he could get a date with me. I was not very receptive, so he thought I'd never call him.

I first met Ron at Leonard's house, where Ralph and I were participating in group therapy. Ron wasn't in our group, but was there to talk to Leonard. We were introduced. I didn't think any more about him, but he must have been attracted to me. Pam knew him and thought highly of him. He was a counselor and worked teaching criminal justice. By the time I called him, he had decided to stick it out with his third wife rather than remarrying.

In my next dream, I find a large green field that looks like a park. Forest surrounds the edges of the field. I look up into a blue sky and see a flock of snow geese circling to land near me. Swooping down and landing, they strut around flapping their big wings and arching their long necks. Then, one by one, they take off again going airborne. In wonderment, I watch each departure. When it comes to the last goose, I notice she is not a goose but a woman! From her neck down to her waist she is covered with small, curly feathers. I can see the shape of her breasts under the feathers as she prepares to follow the other geese.

I think to myself, *Oh, my beautiful love bird, you find one soul mate for your entire life. Great must be your sorrow when your mate can no longer fly at your side.*

I think I was beginning to experience a sense of loss of my own mate and wondering whether I'd ever find another husband. "The times are a changing" as Bob Dylan sang.

More changes, as I look out our west living room window in another dream. I see a beautiful, silvery airplane with a very unique design, fly low overhead. I recognize Ralph's father Bob and his second wife Jeanne in the plane. Ralph has joined me and they wave at us as Ralph and I excitedly watch them fly by. We go outside to see where the airplane has gone. I scan our back plowed field, but now see a very different plane has landed briefly in our back field. It's a yellow jet. The jet prepares to take off again.

I'm concerned there won't be enough runway space for the yellow jet to get airborne. It comes across the field toward me, and just in the nick of time, rises off the ground! I look in the direction it's headed. Our neighbor's barn is in the jet's path. I'm worried the plane won't get high enough to clear the barn. The plane collides into it, slicing off the top half and carrying it into the field. There the weight of the barn drags the jet to a halt. The jet comes out from under the barn roof. It now has a cable wrapped around the upper half of the barn. The jet tows it back to the rest of the barn, so the damage can be repaired. I know our neighbor Don is going to be upset. I walk over to the wrecked barn. The pilot, two couples and a few other people come out of the jet. They start assessing the damage and what work will have to be done to repair it. I'm not sure they will be successful.

As I ponder this dream, I thought of Ralph's father Bob and Jeanne who came into the nursery partnership with us in an up-beat attitude, similar in characteristics of a silvery, new- aged plane. Their log house was on a hill behind us and the next property over. I suspect the dream showed the break-up of the partnership after our divorce. The barn representing the nursery. Yellow jet: a fast departure that demonstrates all kinds of problems with the partnership. I heard Ralph and his father almost got into a law suit over the settlement of the tree farm, then Bob backed down. I was out of the picture at that time.

My next dream, Ralph and I are traveling out on a forested country road to his brother Doug's house. As the road comes to a small lake, we find massive road construction. Dirt has been pushed around and dumped in different places, far from being finished. We get out of the car and walk over the loose dirt. Ralph frowns and tightens his jaw. He doesn't like the changes in the road, but he's determined to find another way to Doug's house on foot.

We've come to the top of a small hill, down below are three farms with flat green pasture extending behind each place. A road runs in front of the farm houses. Ralph says that this is the pathway he wishes to go. I see a wide imaginary path leading straight across the back of the three farms. I don't like this way, because we'll be trespassing on other people's land and privacy. Ralph won't be detoured. His mind is made up. I anxiously follow about two steps behind him.

As we cross the first field, we are met by a brown Doberman Pinscher who circles us growling a warning. I'm afraid of being attacked and I step in closer to Ralph. Ralph is unconcerned by the dog and hardly notices him, ignoring the snarls. Ralph keeps his eyes straight ahead and he doesn't break stride. The Doberman decides to let Ralph pass, since he is not intimidated, but follows right behind me, waiting for me to lag behind Ralph's protective force. The guard dog snaps at my free swinging hands, so I pull them closer to my body to avoid his jaws, keeping in tight step with Ralph.

We have passed through the back fields and are coming to a fence. I decide I've been hassled enough by this dog. I'm going to challenge him. I quickly turn, grabbing the Doberman's head and falling on top of the dog, pinning him to the ground. He doesn't utter a sound, not such a fierce dog now, but I'm left holding him down, so he won't get back up and fight. Then I see a little white poodle dancing across the field toward me. The poodle comes right up to me and whispers something in my ear. On hearing what the poodle says, all that has happened seems unimportant to me. I let go.

I find myself in Doug and Tam's kitchen with blue counter tops. They have a lot of windows and I see the forest outside. Maybe it's a log cabin, because I haven't been in their house before. Perhaps in reality it really does look like this.

The road in the dream showed the changes going on in Ralph's relationship with his brother Doug. Finding Doug's house will take forgiveness for both of them. I'm concerned about the way Ralph is going about it. When I stood up for myself against the intimidating Doberman, I was rewarded. The white poodle was God sent. I was blessed by arriving at Doug's house. The blue counters where you prepare your food represented spirituality. The forest was Doug's love of outdoors and his privacy.

Chapter Twenty-Two

In my dream I'm having a reaction to a particular circumstance. At the end of the dream, I'm alone in a section of an old city thinking about what has just transpired. Suddenly, a much larger world of understanding is opening for me. It reveals all the purposes and meanings of my current dream, and why I just relived this event. I'm now feeling caught up and at one with my destiny.

I see spirits flying and zipping through the air. They are white transparent forms with human faces and bodies, except their legs and feet look like the tails of comets.

I'd finished reading the book by Jane Roberts called SETH SPEAKS. In the book Seth describes our real bodies of light which is just what I think I saw in the dream! I liked this book because Seth spoke of God as "All There Is", another way of looking at the all-powerful creator. A good approach for people who have wandered away from the idea of a God. I was interested in what Seth described on the inside of us and how our planet of people had become too ego oriented, like an unbalanced dictator, limiting who we are as people.

Now I'm going to go back to another dream where I see I'm not the person I was in high school. I'm traveling by car with my parents. We are going on a trip together. Along the way, we stop and pick up my sister, Linda, who will accompany us. At a road side park, we stop and take a break. As we prepare to leave in our car, I see one of my high school class mates Beverly across the road. I lean out the car window and call out to her in a warm, friendly manner. She strolls over to me and we engage in an animated conversation.

In high school, I wouldn't have talked to this popular person. Then, I would have been afraid I didn't have anything interesting, let alone something in myself worth sharing and being happy to express. So what's the big fear? Usually rejection, I surmised because my older sister Linda was quite unfriendly to me. She acted as though she didn't want me around. So I just got used to it. I didn't share much, unless it was with my friend Diana. I felt safe with her. We had fun and could complete each other's sentences. I didn't have many friends, and the ones I did have, I was very close with them.

Let's also go back again to the mountain top dream. In that dream I was blown off the top of it. Here's another mountain dream with different results. I find myself at the top of a small rock mound, maybe 30 feet tall. I'm sitting cross-legged and meditating. I notice a dark haired man in a suit approach my mountain. He stops at the foot, facing me. Then he spreads out both arms wide and bows to me like he might be worshiping me! I think, *he must be putting me on*. I feel uncomfortable, unworthy to have someone bow down to me. I slide off my mountain.

Here, in this dream, I found myself doing what one should do at the top of a mountain, mediate and discover the glory of the Universe. The man was showing me his appreciation. I finally got it! Though, I still have further to go to appreciate my own self-worth, symbolized to me as a small mountain.

To continue on in the spiritual frame, the next dream seems to be a past life dream. I find myself sitting on a stone bench in the foyer of a huge cathedral. I'm all alone, just taking in the gorgeous, magnificent construction of the church. It must have taken many lifetimes for the workers to complete. On the back wall of the entranceway are sculptured pillars reaching way up to support the ceiling. At about waist height is a bas-relief wall decoration stretching along the same wall. As I look up higher on the wall, there appears on the right side, a cluster of white robed Holy Men and angels moving together across the wall. Coming from the other direction is a smaller group of withered men with animal heads crawling toward the Holy

Men and angels. It appears as though they are all going to collide. As the two groups meet, there's an explosion of white light. The Holy Men and angels reappear intact and the animalistic men have gone. I think what a marvelous example of enacted art work for the church and its people.

Next, I'm standing outside a country house in the woods. I'm surrounded by a dozen soldiers on horseback. The captain is a dark haired man with a mustache and goatee. He's wearing a metal armored helmet, Spanish in style. He says to me, "I'm taking you back to the church where you are needed."

Somehow, I think this has to do with the vision I saw on the cathedral wall. I'm to testify, or act as a representative and living proof of the event. I'm not too happy about being used this way. However, I resign myself to this fate. Why not, I'm not doing anything urgent. I tell the captain I will go with him. I quickly slip off my bra from under my clothes. The captain doesn't understand what I've just done, so questions me. I just smile. He announces I'm to be taken back in a white homespun robe. We stop at a nearby stream for me to bath and dress. The captain is nervous that everything be done correctly as planned. As I go down to the stream, a lieutenant near me whispers, "I won't watch, if you want to run away and hide in the forest." I consider his suggestion.

The dream seemed to be about a past life when I had psychic powers and consented to give myself to the church. The bra thing was a mix-up of time realities in my mind. I was offered a choice to run away, but probably would have been tracked down. I didn't want to be taken tied up! I don't know if I liked that lifetime or not, but I probably had to stay with the church. Maybe it added to my desire to know what I believed.

I can now articulate some new discoveries about my dreams. While dreaming, I'm aware I'm playing all the roles or characters, even though I'm sometimes two very different personalities. A cast of one! Who else would know the most meaningful dramas for myself, than myself? My higher-self was working with me. I had forgotten who I was, because of being so wrapped up in what I thought was so and the realities of Earthy struggles.

I dream Ralph and I are approached by a man who is showing us an old rundown house that needs to be remodeled and fixed for sale. We are to be the freelance remodelers. We stand in a combination living room and dining room. Everything is covered by a blanket of dust. There's a scattering of old furniture left behind by the last owners. I notice an antique pump organ sitting in the living room. It doesn't look spectacular, though it could be rather nice after it was refinished. The whole house has taken a beating over the years and is out of date with old wallpaper and worn linoleum floors.

As the man is preparing to leave us with our tasks, I say, "May I have first choice on buying the organ, if I decide I would want it?" He agrees. I continue looking around the place some more. I stare at a white pedestal sink in the middle of the dining room. What a strange place for a bathroom sink. I walk into a big kitchen without cupboards and a counter. Where the table should be, there's another bathroom sink like the other one and by it is a dirty toilet without a toilet seat. The only kitchen sink I can find is a small bathtub beside the stove. I open a door off the kitchen. I'm relieved to find a bathroom intact with the same toilet. I'm confused by the other sinks and toilet in the wrong places. I decide to get started cleaning. I go back into the living room and begin to scrape the wallpaper off the walls. Gradually, I come to some black paper that's covering a door. I peel this off and discover a paned glass door. It leads into a nice master bedroom. I like this room. Then I go back and continue peeling off wallpaper and I find another door. This door opens into a children's room with twin beds. There are two rag dolls lying on the floor, and near the two dolls is a twisted white rag like a handkerchief. I don't want to touch it, but the room needs to be cleaned, so I pick it up. It turns out to be the white aprons for the rag dolls.

I exit the children's room and decide next to dust and clean the old organ. As I rub the surface of the organ, it becomes more and more beautiful. The marred wood changes into a lovely, red stained mahogany. The mantel piece turns out to be a hand carved piece. It has a flower vase at its center in the shape of a winner's cup with carved leaves around it. This matches the organ in every way. It's definitely a collector's item now!

I have an idea about the kitchen bathtub, so I go back to take another look. I think Ralph could mount a hand-pump on it, so it could be used as a kitchen sink. But would he do it? The organ enters my mind again; thinking about how nice it would be to have music. Then I hear wonderful sounds coming from the living room. I walk in and see a woman in her fifty's playing the organ with skill. I stand to her left, watching her.

The fixer-upper house was a hint about what Ralph and my relationship needed; a new way of looking at old worn-out ideas and habits and changing them. Sinks in the wrong places; mainly eating places, should be where cleaning of hands or purification needed to be done. The dirty toilet without seat stood for elimination of shitty ways in our lives not released. As I worked on the walls, or myself, new rooms open for my use. My love of the organ is pointing to my spiritual self. The more you polish it, the more beautiful you become, producing lovely music to live by in happiness. Ralph seemed to not be around after the beginning of the dream. He wasn't helping with the work, which suggested to me, he didn't want to change. Finding the rooms could have meant I would eventually continue in a marriage with family life. The dolls' apron might have been about children needing to do the work of keeping their rooms clean and organized. But a relationship takes two people working together to solve problems and I appear to be alone in this.

Chapter Twenty-Three

    I'm hesitant to go forward into the next chapters because I'll be discussing problems in my marriage that generated fear and anger in me, as does the prospect of divorce for most people. The dreams will show this.

    I dream that I arrive at a newly constructed office building. The building is owned by two partners, who are just moving in. One of the partners is showing me around and explaining the workings of the office. He tells me his business partner has cheated him out of some of their mutual funds. I see the cheating partner has moved into an upstairs suite where he sits on his bed.

    We enter his room. The partner I'm with has a knife in his hands. He says, "We should castrate this partner." My role will be to assist in this punishment. The cheating partner is lying on his back on the bed naked from the waist down. I push his legs up against his chest. His penis is hidden between his thighs and his balls are sucked-up tight against his body, not very accessible for my accomplice with the knife. The man I'm holding isn't making much of a fuss, just wiggling around and whining about how difficult it is to go through this. We move to the other side of the bed where we now have him in position to remove his balls. The man I'm clutching begins wretching; sick to his stomach and prepares to vomit. I become disgusted with the whole scene. I decide this castration is not worth the effort!

This dream is not about money, but sexual cheating between married partners. My ego brought up the dark anger and likes punishments. Cutting off the balls would destroy the sexual desire, but then it wouldn't help the cheating partner to learn control over himself and faithfulness to another. Marriage vows are important. You will suffer when you cheat, though you may think you're getting away with something. As the song says, "Your cheating heart will tell on you." If you are cheating, you cannot truly love and respect yourself. Was my ego testing me to see if I'd go through with the castration? I'm glad I didn't.

There are values in my life I would fight to preserve. I sometimes am surprised when incidents pop up challenging my values. I've had to become stronger with enforcing what I wanted to happen or not to happen. As my life continues, I go to extremes in being tough. It takes giving up your weakness and trying to find the right balance.

In my next dream Ralph and I are at Snoqualmie Pass ski resort where we plan to have fun riding the chair lift together. As we approach the ski lift, the operator says to me, "You should check in your purse at the desk, so you won't lose it on the ride. You need both hands to hold on. All the skiers do this." I remember I had ridden the chair lift before with my bag and I'd done just fine, but I decide to take his advice and check in my purse.

When I reach the counter, three other young ladies on the other side of the counter are picking up their purses. They are done for the day. I lay my handmade, sheepskin purse I'd fashioned for myself, down on the counter. The three other ladies take their purses and leave. I look back down at the counter and my purse is gone! The man at the desk tries to show me some other bags he thinks might be mine. "No, that's not my purse or my number." I realize, the young ladies have stolen my purse! I'm not going to stand for that. I turn and race after them. I catch them at the checkout gate. I'm outraged and ready to fight for my beloved wool purse. I confront the women, demanding my stolen bag back. "No one is going to leave until I have it back." I grab the third lady as she tries to get away. I see my purse hanging over her back. While we wrestle for it, she throws it over the fence by the gate. I let her go and dash for my sheepskin bag, but the second lady gets to my bag first, snatching it up and running away with it. I'm right behind her when she slips on some snowy ice and lands flat on her back, hurting herself. I pick up my fallen purse and brush the snow off, thinking to myself, *she got what she deserved by trying to steal my bag.*

I'm still quite angry when the first young woman comes up to me and says, "At least you don't have to be so nasty about the whole thing." I spin around and sock her right in the mouth. I walk back to the ski lift to try the ride again, only this time, I'm not letting go of my lovely, handmade purse.

So, here we have righteous indignation on my part. I feared personal lose. Attack didn't make me happy, even though I had my purse back. I was strong, but not a happy strength. I was fighting for my integrity. Later in life, I learned that seeing a fearful world was an attack on my invulnerability. I'm safe and loved, perhaps I have somethings that need working out, but I don't need to be fearful while going about it. We can never lose anything of real importance. What God has given to us, can't be taken from away, so says THE COURSE IN MIRACLES.

On the other hand, a dream can show me some small things I need to attend to in my daily life. In this dream, I'm sitting at a table with a man who is holding my hand, as he uses a cuticle stick to push back the skin growing over my lower fingernails. I notice my cuticles are in pretty bad shape with skin split and torn around the edges of the nails. This man has taken on the job of doing this task for me. I'm apprehensive and fidgety because my cuticles are very sensitive. Even though the man is being careful as he pushes, it hurts. I wish he'd hurry up and complete the manicure.

After writing down that dream, I searched for our fingernail cleaning set and manicured my nails.

I found a dream about my ex-brother-in-law, Tom. He was married to Ralph's sister Betty. They had three sons. The first son died when he was five years old of a malignant brain tumor. Everyone took the passing of Daniel very hard.

In the dream Tom and I are happily going to attend a large reception and cocktail party. It is located on the second floor of a building complex which seems to occupy the same block where my parents live. The two places overlap on the same spot, which is strange to me.

In Earth life, Tom would later come into Seattle to visit his two sons. Before leaving, he stopped at our place for a visit. Ralph and I were fond of Tom and enjoyed his company, though Betty didn't think we should like him after their divorce. I took Tom to the airport the next morning in our van. On the ride, Tom confided to me that Ralph had told to him he was going to divorce me. Tom felt I should be forewarned. On returning home, I didn't reveal what Tom had told me. I continued to work on planning a party at my painting and jewelry studio for that weekend, where some of our best friends and acquaintances were invited.

At my studio party Ralph announced he was going to divorce me. I happened to be holding a white Styrofoam drink cup in my hand. I threw it right in his face, as I crushed the cup in my hand! It was so reminiscent of my past dream where he was playing around with another woman. Needless to say, he ruined my party. Everyone felt very uncomfortable after his statement.

My next dream intensifies my feelings. I'm in an isolated dry, barren place with some low rolling hills and sagebrush. I'm at the workplace of a man who has an old shack and tool yard with cyclone fencing around them. The man points to the west and says, "A typhoon is brewing. It's headed our way. We must go and cling with all our strength to the cyclone fence, so we won't be blown away!" The man goes and stretches himself with his back against the fence and his fingers and feet intertwined in the wire links. I hurry and copy him, along with another man who is on the other side of me. Tom's children and mine are with their grandmother Ruth, Ralph's mom, in a manmade foxhole a stone's throw away from me. They will be out of the force of the wind. I look into the distance at a dark, dusty sky. We are hit by three strong gusts of wind. It takes all my strength to just hold on and not be blown away! The man to my left, partially loses his grip. We recover and adjust our bodies, but the property owner say, "That was just some mild gusts, the center of the storm has not yet arrived."

I'm worried and frightened that I won't be able to hold on. I could barely cling on in the last smaller gusts. Yet, I want with all my heart not to be blown away. I say a prayer out loud. "Please, God protect me from the wind. Make me cling tightly so I won't be destroyed." All my intention and energy goes into this prayer. I see my energy flowing out from me in a straight intense line. We brace for the oncoming gale winds. Then I see Sonia crawl out of their foxhole and mess around with something around the edge of it. I yell, "Get back into your hole!" She slowly crawls back in, only to climb out the other side. I'm angry with her for fooling around in the face of danger. Grandmother Ruth seem unaware of Sonia's recklessness. She sits huddled in the hole with the other grandchildren. I scream, "Get into that hole and stay there!" Then the storm hits us directly. I'm surprised that the wind is mild making it easy for me to hold on to the cyclone fence. I look around at the others and they aren't having any difficulty either. My prayers were answered!

I woke up, amazed by being shown the power of prayer in my dream. I felt so happy! Not only did it help me, but the others in the dream as well. I remembered that dream throughout my life. I know if I call on Him with passion, God will help me. In the dream the storm was the brewing divorce. I would survive a divorce that had one of everything in it, child custody, property disputes, and who would get my studio. It took a year to complete.

To continue on with my thoughts at this time in my life, I had some crushing feelings brought to awareness by this next dream. I'm out on a prairie in a dry bush country. There're a few scrubby trees on the rolling plain. I'm crouched behind some bushes as I'm currently engaged in an Indian ambush. I've just fought off some attackers and am feeling confident about my abilities to defend myself. I look down at my body and discover that I'm a young brave of deep skin color, muscular and of medium height. I turn, as another young Indian man, wearing only a loincloth, creeps up behind me. He leaps, stabbing me near the heart and ripping a long, gashing wound. He quickly bounds away.

I'm not as aware of the pain as I am the force of the knife that opened the wound. I clasp my hands tightly over the deep rip in my chest, feeling my slippery throbbing heart exposed against my palms. My only thought is to get away from the battle, as now I'm unable to defend myself. I stagger through the underbrush, pressing firmly against my chest wound. I don't think about death, but escape. I'm not sure what's keeping me going, maybe shock. I manage to swing up on my horse and ride away. I notice a piece of my intestine is exposed. I try not to think of my injuries.

I feel weary and tired as my horse picks her way across a wide, shallow river. I'm coming up the other bank when I'm met by two white trappers or maybe scouts. They immediately want to take advantage of me as I sag under my fatal wound. One wants to shoot me and stop my retreat. The other man is opposed to this. A loud argument erupts between them. I'm forgotten as they draw their guns on each other.

My view point has moved from the wounded warrior to the middle of the river, where I have a better view of the angry Bushmen. I feel relief for the dying Indian who can now ride away, free to continue his journey home. The men have turned against each other.

Stabbed in the heart was how I was feeling in my life. A war of attack only creates fatalities. How could I get through my disillusion about love? I desire my peace of mind again. Real love ought to be stronger than this. The COURSE IN MIRACLES talks about our special love we make. I love you if you do what I want and hate you when you don't.

As my relationship stormed, I felt like I was wading waist deep in surging, swampy waters. I needed to find a church family for myself. I ask my new astrology teacher whether she knew of a good church. Her answer was, "Yes, Unity of Bellevue." I went alone to this church the following Sunday. Sitting in the pew with others, I felt surrounded by love! If I didn't hear any words that were said, I at least bathed myself in love. I needed that love so much.

Now to lighten up with my next dream; I'm standing by a framed in area filled with a small mound of shiny black coal that sits on the floor in the center of the room. A couple of people are with me. I can't figure out why I'm stuck here looking at coal. So, with my mind, I splash water to wash over it. Then I remember I can create what happens to me. So, in jest, I dump chocolate pudding in the place of the coal. At this, I laugh and jump into the middle of it. I roll in the messy chocolate and have a great time! This activity arouses some sexual feeling in my body.

I thought this dream was showing me I have plenty of fuel to use in my life, so I'd better get to work. However, I remember my power and decide to have some fun first, to laugh at myself after all I've been through.

Chapter Twenty-Four

    We all know that parents' behaviors effects their children. They often model some of their actions and attitudes after us: sometimes not in the ways we would like. This can cause us to make changes in our behavior and situation.

    In my next dream Ralph and I are on the coast near some big shelters where a large group of people are staying. A few of these people come up to us and ask if we would like to participate in a sex orgy they're going to have. I say, "No." I feel no interest in this kind of event. Ralph shakes his head, too. I turn and walk away.

    After I leave, Sasha and Sonia approach Ralph and ask, "Can we go? Can we go?"

    Ralph answers, "I guess it's alright, if you want to go." Our girls turn and run after the people.

    When I return, I ask Ralph, "Where have the girls gone?"

    He says, "I told them they could go to the orgy."

    I'm shocked, "Why did you tell them that?" I rush off after our daughters, for they are much too young to be involved in something like this. I find the group has left a large shower house and traveled by raft to a nearby island. I stand on the shore and scan the island with my senses allowing me to know if my girls are there or not, without having to see them. They are not there. I turn and walk to the shower house. The building is dark and hollow sounding. I don't want to enter, but I hear some voices coming from inside. I know they're in there and have stayed behind with a couple of other people. I call into the bath house, "Sasha and Sonia I want you to come out here right now!" I feel nervous and worried. They answer me, but take a long time to come as though they're in no hurry. We take hands and walk back to where we were staying.

When we get back, I'm pretty mad at Ralph for letting the girls go. I have our divorce papers in my hands. Ralph says, "Well, make-up your mind. Are you going to sign or not?" I sign the papers. I know I really don't want a divorce and Ralph also knows this. I reluctantly hand the papers to Ralph, who takes them and runs off.

I call after him, "Wait, we have a lot of unfinished business!" I'm not sure what he is going to do now. I follow after him. I see him meet with Arlene, one of his woman friends.

He says to Arlene, "I won't be seeing you anymore, and don't tell your two boys right away.

I'm pissed off about Ralph's involvement with her. I turn and go off to find Leonard our marriage therapist. When I get to Leonard's house, I see Arlene sitting on his couch with her back to me. I Say, "Oh, shit," and another cuss word very loudly. I whip around and stomp off.

I almost bump into a man who asks me, "What are you so up-set about?"

I answer, "I don't know whether I'm married or not." Then I decide to return the way I've came and find Ralph. Passing through Leonard's living room, I see Arlene is now sitting on a stool near the door. Beyond the door is Ralph. I snort, thinking how I will have to pass Arlene to get to Ralph. I crouch and start to run, as I approach Arlene my anger accelerates. I deliberately smash her with my shoulder, knocking her sprawling off the stool. I don't even look back. I head straight out the door and begin talking to Ralph.

Arlene comes out the door after me. She says, "What was that all about?"

I retort, "I'm very angry at you!" Ralph tries to put his arm between us. I say, "Mind you own business. This is between the two of us." I grab of her neck and shoulders and everything resolves into slow motion as my anger reaches full blown. This is a distortion caused by my anger which seems to be taking a long time to reach capacity. I have her now and she's not going to get away until I've vented myself. Arlene acts indignant and tries to rationalize her way out of my attack. I yell insults at her. I'm so mad that I can't even think of more nasty words! Then I remember, I can hit her, so I land some blows to her head. I throw her to the floor and sit on top of her holding her arms down with my knees. She is no match for my strength.

I want to think of something awful to do to her. I look around and see a drinking fountain near us. I drag her over, holding her down with one arm while I turn on cold water and let it run over her. Still not satisfied, I remember the arm lock that hurts a lot. I flip her over and twist her arm behind her back, while yelling, "You are trying to steal my old man, aren't you!"

"No, no, no," she hollers back, again trying to wiggle free. She sounds like she thinks I'm crazy to think of such a thing. When I'm satisfied she's telling the truth. I let go of her, losing all interest in the battle.

Shortly, thereafter, I wakened with a strong tension in my head like an emotional hang-over. The ache lightened as I told Ralph, who was still sharing our bed, about my dream. I admit that I enjoyed the thought of beating her up. Anger will come out. You can suppress it for a while, but it will blow. Dreams are a safe place to work out your problems, so no one gets killed, even though it might look like they went down. You can get in touch with your hostile feelings. That is why it's important to forgive right away, if you know the value of forgiveness. I hadn't learned that yet, as to what forgiveness really was, or that "Attack will bring you nothing you would want," from THE COURSE IN MIRACLES. I will later learn about that.

The dream also reminded me of fights I'd had with my older sister when we were kids. She'd sit on top of me; holding my arms down with her knees and made a big wad of spit to slowly drool on me; childish behavior.

Knowing what I know now, as women, we need to join together and support each other by not messing with other women's husbands, even if they encourage you. Married men are off limits.

You could disappoint a lot of innocent people, and do you want the wrath of another woman? Don't go in that direction unless you want unhappiness or need to learn about revenge.

Asleep again, I'm at a small, white train station out on a prairie. There's a set of railroad tracks running in front of the station. I ask the station master who lives at the station, "When is the next train coming?"

He replies, "The train is coming now," and points to my left, at a train speeding across the plain toward us. I look down the tracks in the direction of the oncoming train. I see the station master's small son has left his toys on the tracks where he was playing. They will be destroyed under the wheels of the approaching engine. I look in the opposite direction and spot another train coming from the south on the same track. The two trains will surely collide head on!

I scan the distances to judge whether I have enough time to knock the toys off the track before the crash. I run over, sweeping the toys clear of the rails with my arms. I scramble up, fleeing as fast as I can away from the tracks. I'm terrified and want to put as much distance away from the collision as I can. I glance over my shoulder, as I race across the dry grass. I watch as the two trains swish past each other on separate tracks, speeding on to their separate destinations. I'm so relieved to realize there were two sets of tracks.

I was reminded how Ralph and I each had our own destinations in life, even if it seemed that we would crash into each other. I needn't fear, there was a track for each of us.

My next dream finds me kneeling in our bed. Ralph is lying on his back in the bed, holding his knees against his chest. He's wearing his boxer shorts that have a large hole in the crouch seam. I'm sitting between his hoisted legs, meticulously hand sewing the big rip closed.

On recording that dream, I smile. *Do you think this will keep his penis inside?* At least, he was agreeable to the repair.

My dream takes me aboard a cabin cruiser driven by Ralph. We are out in the ocean. He has the line of his heavy duty, fishing pole out in the water to catch a fish. I watch his pole bend heavily downward under the strain of a big fish, who's taken his bait. I yell,

"You've hooked a fish!" Ralph grabs the pole and starts reeling hard, not letting up on the fish.

This doesn't seem correct to me. You should pull up on the pole, then quickly reel in the slack and begin again. You let the fish play itself out slowly, as you bring the exhausted fish toward the boat for netting or gaffing. I tell Ralph this, but he continues to try to force the fish straight toward the boat. I sigh, resigning myself. He will have to find out for himself.

Then Ralph starts the boat going full speed ahead and pulling against the fish. I look where we are going as we barely miss hitting a couple of other fishing boats. This frightens me, so I close my eyes telling Ralph to stop the boat!

Ralph brings the boat in and docks it. I guess the first fish was lost. He now decides to fish from the dock. He gets another hit on his line, but loses it trying to bring it in.

As I thought about that dream, I decide that Ralph should not dominate, just because he was big and strong, against fish or other people. It's a courting game. See if your interests are going in the same direction, if not, it won't last. Self-centeredness won't bring you relationships. It's about two people in a mutual give and take in a dance of hearts seeking their own ways through life. Can we ride side by side or will we split off? There are always rules or guidelines to help us stay on track, the structures of society preserving family.

Here's a little sequel to my dream at the start of this chapter. I'm walking toward my house when Pam and her man friend Barney drive-up. They tell me they've been to a movie where Arlene played the leading role. One of them asks me if I know the famous actress.

I say, "Yes, I know her, but Ralph knows her better." I don't seem to feel any malice toward her, only surprise that she is famous.

Chapter Twenty-Five

My dreams are now shifting more to myself as I continue on with my dreams. I'm standing in the backyard of my parents' house where I grew-up. A section of our tall, backyard fence is missing on the alley side. Framed in the opening, a beautiful pony with long white mane and forelock appears. She is standing in tall, wind-swept grasses. These blades of grass have soft white seeds that float like milkweed and are scattered over the curved grass stems. I'm amazed and pleased to find the pony in my own backyard. I will care for it.

I've always loved horses. To me, they were like close friends and would take me places I desired to go. White is a spiritual color. The pony will assist me on my inner journeys. A pony, because I'm just getting started on finding what I believe in.

My father is with me in my next dream. We are in a gym with a stage at one end. There're a few other people milling around. I'm talking to my father as we stand by the stairs leading to the right side of the stage. I'm telling him that I sense the presence or energy of an invisible person in this gym. My father disputes this as he doesn't believe in this sort of thing.

Immediately, I'm swooped up into the air by the energy of this spirit. I sail along on my bottom toward the ceiling then back down. My father watches in amazement! The ride doesn't scare me, as I've flown before under my own power. It's not foreign to me, but I find the force a bit tippy and erratic, since I don't know what direction it will go. Now, I see it's taking me across the room where I'm about to collide into the top of a beautifully decorated Christmas tree standing at the side of the gym. I exert my own air breaks and hop down to the floor. I'm pleased with my solution to the problem. I say to Dad, "See, I can use some of my will power to control this unseen energy."

My father and I walk over to a high table stand on which a candle is burning. The invisible person focuses its energy into the candle. The candle quickly begins to change forms several times in width, length and color. Then it completely melts, spreading out on the table with the small wick still burning in the center. I say, "See, spirits can start fires and shouldn't go unwatched."

I'm now in a car headed toward an old three story house to attend a meeting. As I arrive, I know the spirit person is in one of the upstairs windows. I desire to get a glimpse of him as we drive by. At first, I don't see anything, but then I notice a white mist in one of the upper windows. I can barely make out a shadowy form within the whiteness.

Inside the house on one of the upper floors, I feel confident knowing this presence is also here like a special secret. The meeting I'm going to attend will be interesting.

On reviewing this dream, I'm not sure what to say about the spirit energy. When I was first married and lived behind Cannery Row. I met a homeless young woman named Kerry. She was staying in an empty cannery building. As I befriended her, she told me she'd seen ghosts in the building. I'd heard it was used as a whorehouse at one time. Probably it was a confused, deceased person lingering earth bound over some tragedy that needed forgiveness or discovery. I think perhaps that ghosts want to get our attention but won't hurt us, as they come from a different level of stuck awareness.

Maybe I should have spoken to that energy in my dream to see what it wanted. Though to be invisible, is to be evasive. I still detected its presence. I've not seen a ghost in my waking life, although my father had a neighbor who had his house torn down because he said there were ghosts in it. We happen to own the house next to that property now.

I dream I'm in a car that has stopped at a view point, where I can look down over white cliffs to a tropical blue ocean with fishing boats afloat. Someone is narrating about the fishing events below. I look across from my passenger's seat and see a man in the driver's seat. He is doing the talking. He opens his car door so he has a better view for describing what's happening below. I feel fear about falling out of the car and over the cliffs.

The scene shifts and I'm standing near the water below next to my dark haired driver. He has just caught a huge fish. I see the fish dangling on this line above the water. The fish is bigger than me! I want to know what he's going to do with his fish. I ask him, "Are you going to eat the fish?" (I'm determined to get an answer.) He didn't respond.

Jesus said, "Come follow me and I will make you fishers of men." (Mt 4:190) Now, women are included, too. Has he caught me? What will I be doing for him, spread the truths of heaven? Live on Earth as it is in heaven?

Chapter Twenty-Six

When I married and left home, I still had two brothers who were seven and eight and a half years younger than myself who lived with Mom and Dad. According to my father, as my brothers reach teenage, the police in Pasco liked to harass these boys living in town. Both of my brothers had motorcycles and were chased out in the country by the police. They even fired on them once. My father had trouble controlling his temper and these events and discipline problems started him drinking. Mother, who invited a policeman to visit her first grade room each year, was shocked to see they sometimes weren't good guys. It threatened her belief-system.

My next dream addresses some of this. I'm with Mom and Dad on a camping trip at a lake, when Dad decides to take Mom to go out drinking for the evening. I'm not interested in drinking, so I don't go with them.

The next morning, as I walk up the sidewalk to my parents' front door, I notice all sorts of debris scattered around the front yard. This makes the yard seem uncared for by my parents. I feel displeasure at the site of the mess. When I enter the house, I find everything in disarray, as if the house hadn't been cleaned for some time. My father hurries downstairs from his bedroom and begins hastily washing the dirty dishes. He says, "The mess was because I'd been out drinking so late. I needed to sleep most of the day in order to get enough rest."

I feel he's just giving me another excuse about part of himself he's unwilling to change. I glance around at the dirty living room and think to myself, *"Why do you pain me with this mess, for you know how I dislike seeing your personal negligence."*

In this case, my insight came right within the dream, my disappointment with my dad.

My father did come to Fall City to help me with the building of my studio. He was a carpenter and had air guns that would make the construction go faster, plus he paid for the nails. Every night we had to push him up the ladder to the attic where he was sleeping because he consumed a fifth of bourbon in the evenings. He didn't drink during the day so as not to interfere with his work.

The next dream takes Sonia and me on a mother-daughter field trip with her school class. We are aboard a large ferry and we are sitting next to Sonia's teacher, Mrs. Jones. Across the aisle from us, I notice a fair-haired man with a banjo. His musical instrument is quite ornate with metal scroll work set with colored stones. I'm pleased he's here on the boat, perhaps he'll play some music for us. I point him out to Sonia. He smiles and begins to play us a song. As he strums his banjo, the instrument changes into different music instruments, like an autoharp and Dobro. He moves into various positions to play them without missing a beat, quite amazing. Sonia's teacher is very taken with his abilities. He comes over to us and hands me his instrument, which now looks like a stringed instrument played over one's knees while sitting down, a dulcimer. I run my fingers across it in a strum. The musician and Mrs. Jones gaze lovingly into each other's eyes. I continue to pick out a tune, but I see that one of the scroll pieces with the red stone has come off the instrument. I'm concerned about this and I look to see if I can find where it fits. When I have it matched up, I see that a small screw is missing. I look up and say to the others, "It's alright, I can fix it."

The teacher and musician dance off together where they can be alone with their infatuation of each other. When they leave, a mother gets up pulling her daughter behind her. She walks down the aisle towards us complaining and bitching loudly, because the teacher has left. As she nears me, I say in a firm voice, "Why don't you shut-up!"

Thinking about this dream made me realize, we're all having a good time in the dream, until the ego voice of judgement and criticism gets up. I'm glad I didn't buy into it. Music is a great teaching aid and can bring out one's passions. I had forgotten about the power of music to carry me through hard times, so I was handed the banjo that needed a little fixing. I was shown the amazing things any instrument could do by the music man.

I dream I go for a walk through green pastures where I meet some people who give me a gift of a strong Palomino horse! I'm very delighted and pleased these people would do this for me. I mount my gift horse because I want to find out how the animal performs. Ahead of us is a long stretch of rolling green grasses. I give the horse full rein and urge him to show his full energy to run at top speed! The strong muscles of the Palomino surge, as his pounding hooves speed over the fields. The horse and I flatten out with the wind whipping through both our manes. I find it easy to stay on the horse's back. I keep one eye on the ground, as occasionally I see some debris in our pathway and dips in the surface. I want to be aware if the palomino is going to jump, so I can hold on with my knees to absorb the jolt, should he choose this approach. He doesn't, and soon we are home.

I tie a long rope onto the Palomino since I don't have a fenced in pasture. I'm aware this is an unsatisfactory way to keep an animal. I go back out to him. Nearby us is a small, rushing mountain stream with plenty of green grass growing by it. There's no need to tie the horse because food and water are near. He won't wander away. I take the rope off and watch him leisurely graze.

"He maketh me lie down in green pastures, he leadeth me beside still waters, he restoreth my soul. (Ps 23:2) "Surely goodness and mercy shall follow me all the days of my life", (Ps 23:6) comes to my mind here. The run was invigorating. I was given help on my journey to the crossroads of my life.

Coming back to my state od mind, my dream starts with me observing a tall, slim woman with dish-water blond hair. I'm not in a body form. She is arguing with her man friend. I can sense her feelings of frustration and discouragement. The man is also making advances toward her with his sexual desires which she is not sure how to handle. I know her first husband, whom she loved dearly, was killed in a car accident. Since it happened, she hasn't been able to establish a successful love relationship.

The scene changes and the woman is in a room with other people who are participating in a group therapy session. The therapist is a kind, eager man with blondish hair. He has his sleeves rolled-up, and he's encouraging the group members to search to the depths of themselves to find what is really going on, then express it to the group.

I've become a member of the group. I don't want to do this, get into myself right now, let alone, share it with the group. I'm relieved when the husband of another woman speaks out. He begins to talk about his feelings and becomes upset, crying and sobbing about how he hates his body. He's an overweight person. The therapist nods his head in understanding. He was expecting that it was so for this man.

Later, I'm again worried the attention might focus on me, but then, the woman I was watching earlier, begins to tell her story. It's about the most honest, right on story I've ever heard. I quite identified with her problem, but I can't remember it now. I say "Right on", as I reach into my mouth and pull out a loose molar. I inspect the tooth I hold in my fingers.

Someone says to me, "How can you keep losing all those teeth?"

I say, "These aren't my permanent teeth. They are my baby teeth.

I have lost teeth in dreams before, and this dream was giving me a hint at what losing a tooth might mean. I think teeth represent beliefs. I my case, childhood beliefs, part of the fairyland stuff we were raised on with all the how did they live happily ever after left out. I thought I didn't want to look at the part I'd played in my failed relationship. To not look, is to not learn the errors in our thinking so real change can happen. Forgiveness was about shining light on our made-up versions of what we think others have done to us. Then let it go, as not the real truth because we made it up. We need to find God's truth that is real.

A dark, haired man is again leading me in my next dream. We are in the dining room of a nice older wooden house. The man says to me, "You can have a shortbread cookie from the plate on the table, if you want." I feel pleasantly surprised at the suggestion. I double check, whether I heard him right. As I eat my cookie, I really enjoy the sweet, delicate favor.

We walk into the living room, where I see a most unusual Christmas tree. The tree is a Noble Fir with wide spaces between each layer of limbs. Many different colored, medium sized balloons are nestled on the branches and are dusted with powered sugar and flour. I find the tree very artistic and beautifully done. Across the room from the tree is a pile of unwrapped Christmas presents, not under the tree where most people would put them.

To me, a Christmas tree symbolized inner-joy. The sugar coated balloons are not a lasting ornament. They eventually pop or lose air. The gifts not yet under the tree convey the message that they hadn't been received and were still waiting for me. I think I needed to hang more substantial, solid values on the tree to receive the gifts I was meant to have. I was given a taste to interest me, the cookie representing the sweet things in life.

I dream, Ralph and I have just journeyed through a wilderness complete with snowcapped mountains. On our journey we'd found a way down through the pass. Below us runs a wide rushing river in flood stage. The water is brown with silt, churning in turmoil. I know we have to cross the river directly ahead. I lead us to the bank where we jump into the water and start swimming across. I realize the river is flowing in two different directions. We're on the wider, slower moving side that will eventually run into a multi-mouthed, meetings of rivers, then out to sea. This side is easier to maneuver, as long as you keep moving.

When we approach the far side, I see right away that we won't be able to cross here, because the second side is impossible, too narrow, swift and full of rapids. I call to Ralph who is behind me, "We can't cross here. Let's drift downriver a little more to see if we can find a place where the second river spreads out and isn't so rough." We float down a bit, but there isn't much time to drift, as the confluence of the gathering rivers are just ahead. I anxiously call out, "If we're going to cross, we'll have to do it now, so start swimming with all your strength!" Ralph drifts past me down river. I'd hoped he'd make it with me, but now I have to save myself. He'll be on his own to save himself.

Ralph and I had gone through a lot of tough terrain together. Now, we've arrived at a formidable river in flood stage and flowing in two different directions. Will we get to the other side together? No, this is where we are going to split-up, going in our own different directions, still a couple of years away to finality.

Chapter Twenty-Seven

I'm angry and disillusioned with married life. I didn't have much of a handle on my ego-self then. I was always ready to jump in first with the ego's negative voice. The main issue being: I'm the wife who takes care of the house and kids, while Ralph sneaks off chasing other women. I don't want to be the wife, if that is how it works. It looked to me like the mistress was having more fun and no responsibilities. Maybe that role would be better? THE COURSE IN MIRACLE says, nothing comes to you unbidden. As soon as I'd entertained those thoughts, it came upon me. It was after I had custody of the house, while our divorce was pending.

I dream Ron and I have a date to spend the weekend together. I've checked with Ralph if this arrangement is going to be okay with him, and it is. Ralph has taken the weekend off to be with his lady friend before, so this situation isn't unusual for us.

Ralph and I are living on the ground floor of a huge Victorian Hotel, complete with maid service, doorman and managers. The hotel covers one whole block. I walk outside and down the sidewalk on my way to meet with Ron. I see him driving up in an oversized truck, pulling a trailer. The trailer's cargo is two huge, rubber inner tubes, one pink and the other yellow. Ron brings these inner tubes when he takes his dates to the beach. They're a lot of fun to play with in the water.

As Ron pulls up to the curb, two other young women are standing nearby. They quite admire his colored inner tubes and would jump at the chance to go with him. Ron and I drive to his apartment in a hotel and enter in through his private entrance. We kiss and embrace affectionately. We both are in touch with our own sexuality and feel a lot of attraction and respect for each other. There's no need for us to hop-in-the-sack right away for we have all weekend to pick and choose the right time to make love. I can sense that Ron is very pleased about our weekend together. I am feeling all freed-up and completely available to enjoy the time with him. I don't know if he's planned any activities. I'm leaving that part to him.

I experience an inner vision of a tall cruel male who is in charge of the maid services. He is yelling and harassing some of the maids. I find this distasteful and unpleasant and I push it out of my mind.

Ron wants to go for a drive, so that is what we do. We sit close together in the backseat and start making-out. Ron is my style of a kisser, and we are on the same wave length. I'm really digging this, as the kisses get deeper and hungrier. I can feel Ron's hard-on right through his pants, as his hips push against mine, like being screwed with your clothes on. I have a flash of what it would be like to sexually climax with Ron. I imagine Ron's ridged body hovering over mine, moving with hard, long glides, as I observe myself moaning and slowly rolling my head from side to side. I'm pleased that Ron is quite a good lover, perhaps better than Ralph.

I don't want to have sexual intercourse now, in the car. I have become aware that our car is being chauffeured by a matronly woman from the hotel. In the seat next to her is a slender butler, about fifty years old. I wonder if they have been watching us, but they show no sign of it. Their eyes are on the road and the butler is slouched down comfortably in his seat. It's probably their professional duty not to notice what their clients do.

Over the car radio, we hear an announcement, a new man has been appointed to the State Legislature. Ron works in the State Legislature. He sits up, becoming very interested in the broadcast. He wants to go back to his apartment to find out more about this appointment.

When we get back to the hotel, I tell Ron I'm going to walk around the block and come in the front entrance. This is fine with Ron and he enters through his private door. As I walk around the block, I encounter two girls from my high school. They seem to know I'm staying with Ron for the weekend. I think to myself, *they must think my relationship with Ralph has gone bad, and probably think I'm going to get a divorce from him.* As I continue past them, I turn and call back, "By-the way, Ron is just a friend of mine." Then I wonder why I said that, because Ron is not just a friend. I care a lot for him.

At the front doors of the hotel, are many entrances, like gates to an event. You can only get in, if you live here or have business here. I find a place in line at the first gate. I pass through and into the hotel without a problem. As I go down the hall toward Ron's apartment, I see again the mean maid manager who is criticizing the maids and threatening to strike them. They argue back in self-defense. I know the maids are good workers and very conscientious, but this man is extremely picky and impossible to satisfy. He'd find something wrong, even if there wasn't anything undone. I sympathize with the maids.

I continue to Ron's door and go in. I say strongly, "We need to find a way to get rid of the maids' manager!"

Ron listens to me and asks, "How do you want to get rid of him?"

"Fire him, and replace him with someone else." Ron comes over and embraces me affectionately. I become aware again of our attraction to one another. I give him a kiss and go into the bathroom to freshen-up, for we will probably go into the bedroom next. While I'm in the bathroom, the problem of contraceptives comes to my mind. I call to Ron, "My husband has a vasectomy, so I'm not on the pill." I walk out and face Ron, "I'm a fertile woman," Ron smiles and I can tell this information turns him on.

He puts his arm around me and says, "I've got that all taken care of." Then someone knocks on the door. It's a couple of Ron's friends who have stopped by briefly. The man goes over to talk to Ron, something about Ron's work. The woman chats with me.

She asks, "What is your arrangement with Ron?"

I say, "I've agreed to be with Ron for the weekend. It's fine with my husband, as he has arrangements like this, too."

She says, "Including sex?"

I say, "Ralph's dates haven't included sex and I assume anything I want to do is fine." The word assume, really stands out to me. I begin to wonder if I'd assumed something Ralph and I hadn't talked about opening the way to a sticky misunderstanding. I decide I should go back to our hotel at the other end of the block and check this out with him, immediately.

When I arrive at our apartment, Ralph is out. I see that I won't be able to clear this up with him now. I head back toward Ron's place. I feel caught in a dilemma. I don't want to go ahead with Ron and our plans, if it might cause a hassle between Ralph and me. I know Ron and I will be quite disappointed, if I break our date. This conflict in myself ends the dream.

What a confusing situation! I was confused just writing it down. It seems I'm still in a relationship with Ralph, though we live in a hotel, a temporary place in between, in the dream. I don't seem to know what is okay to do with Ron and what is not okay, and somehow I think I need Ralph's approval. This is not how I was feeling when I made my date with Ron. Ron and I never did spend a weekend together. We both had family responsibilities.

With lots of changes happening, I dream of walking into our nursery house backdoor, opening on to the porch, where I first made my jewelry. I immediately notice that Ralph has taken down the curtains I'd made for the porch. I feel a surge of anger because he didn't ask me about this first. I continue into the kitchen/dining room, and it's the same, curtains are all gone. I see the curtain rods still hanging there. One of the rods is missing a screw and dangles downward. I can see daylight coming through the screw hole in the wall. I don't like the way the kitchen looks without the curtains. Again, I'm pissed. He didn't ask me about this either.

I go back to the back porch and jewelry room. I now find a big pile of the family's dirty clothes Ralph has dumped on the floor. I resent this. I hardly have enough room for my small bead shop, let alone all the family's wash. I look at my bench and see a mound of beautiful beads spilled and strangely traveling up the wall.

Ralph comes through the backdoor wanting me to hurry and help him with something. I think to myself, *if I can get enough time I want to pick up the beads, especially the gorgeous flower ones climbing up the wall.* Then I say, "What's the big idea about dumping the wash on the back porch and taking the curtains down!" I feel my anger accelerate.

On thinking about this dream, I hadn't liked the changes to our home, nor did I want demands put on me. I'd rather make jewelry. Ralph had often said to me, "Why don't you get a real job." I guess the dream was showing me I would have to cope with all the dirty clothes dumped in my shop.

I fall back to sleep and dream I'm in a gym taking ballet lessons. All the students are in a large circle around the gym. We are practicing our jumps. I experiment with a few different leaps. I watch the formations of my legs as I soar. Jumping is very pleasing to me. I can stay off the ground as long as I wish to complete the leap. I am particularly satisfied with one jump where I leap off the floor, spreading my legs into full split and rotating them from front to back in a circular motion landing with legs together.

Background changes and we're all in a park close to my parent's home. We are still doing leaps. I'm feel good. I stop and walk across the grass toward my parent's house. As I leave, my dance instructor comes up behind me and embraces me from behind. He has put his arms over my arms so I can't get away or turn around and face him. I like his affections and I want to look him in his eyes. I continue walking forward with him hanging on. I know this person wants to feel my energy, to sense what I'm like. So I radiate my energy flow into his body space.

After a short distance, the dance teacher's grip begins to weaken. I know he will faint from an overdose of power if he doesn't let go. He gasps and releases me. I turn and look at him, as he catches his balance again. He's a tall, fair haired man. He says to me, "You're quite a woman." We walk a ways together. He is on his way to join some friends on a college campus. I know I can't go along with him.

I wonder if my show of strength makes me an undesirable person to be kept in her place.

This dream illustrates more of my feelings and attitudes. I presume to think men don't want strong talented women, probably because most men want to control and lead. Maybe, I'm better off single, though I've never liked living alone. I don't like coming home to an empty house. Who will I talk to and share fun with? Perhaps my practicing jumps points to my eventual need to make a leap when I have to change locations.

I dream Ralph and I are walking across a field, when I playfully jump onto Ralph's back, piggy-back style. Ralph continues to walk along carrying me. I wonder if my weight will bother his back, so I rest my body onto the shelf of his rump. After a bit, Ralph staggers forward, indicating his back is hurting, and he can no longer carry me.

I feel his staggering has to do with finances'. Ralph doesn't want to support a wife anymore. I do like to be provided for; home, food and family.

The next dream of mine, continues this theme. In the dream I see an old classmate of mine, named Kay. She was timid, frail and dependent on others. Kay is standing on the bank of a river. On the other side is a city where all your needs are completely provided. Kay is very excited about going across the river to the City of No Needs. There's one stipulation though, you must have your legs removed from the knees on down. This doesn't deter Kay, she is willing to do this in order to live there.

Ralph asks me, "Do you want to go to the City, too?"

I say, "Part of me does and part of me doesn't. Having part of my legs removed is too final and permanent for me. What if I got tired of the city? It would be almost impossible to get around on this side of the river without working legs?"

Again, part of me would like to be provided for without me having to do all the work to afford a life. The last thing I wanted was to be on my own. However, I would eventually have to face that challenge; the girls and me alone. Of course, there would be child support and money from the property buy-out. I would have to find a full time job, nothing I'm good at, and face being a under paid woman. I'll probably have to pay a job placement company to get a job.

In my next dream I find myself catapulted through the air like I was shot out of a canon. I sail over the top of a cyclone fence landing on my chest and sliding on my belly across the forest floor. With eyes shut, I gradually come to a stop. I feel a scratchy tongue licking my nose affectionately. Opening my eyes I stare into the face of a cougar. Somehow the cougar had been trapped inside the fenced in area. The sight of other people frightens her and she begins to panic.

I want to help the cougar get out of the forest cage. I take her collar and lead her along. It's difficult because the cougar has seen people and is wild-eyed. She's a strong animal, really very gentle and kind, except she doesn't know how to deal with people. On our way out, we pass a doctor's clinic with patients inside. The side door is open so I pull the big cat quickly past, along the outside sidewalk.

An older woman, which I am becoming is sometimes referred to as cougar. I apparently am supposed to save this wild animal, since I was thrown in its direction. I'm leading the cougar by her collar (maybe we are acquainted) toward her freedom and perhaps mine, too. Wild is free of conventions and expected behavior, to become new. The way is never easy, however it is definitely worth the effort. We all love freedom to roam; to become, to act and to create within our true nature.

Chapter Twenty-Eight

As the dreams begins, I'm in a waiting room at the entrance to a huge arena filled with waiting people. A troupe of athletic wonder men are getting ready to go into the arena to perform. They are dressed in tights, belted in jewels and with their arms and chests bare. There're very energetic men, light and springy on their feet. They ask me what they could expect on entering the ring.

My mind flashes forward into the minutes ahead, when they'll be in the arena. I see men planted throughout the crowd with rifles. Half of these wonder athletes will be shot down! I turn soberly toward these gifted men and say, "Half of you will be shot and killed." This grim news doesn't deter them from their intention to entering the arena. I can feel each one of them hopes he will succeed and be one of the lucky ones to survive. I'm saddened by the thought of the death of any of these wonderful men. I can't stand in their way to fulfill the destinies they have chosen for themselves.

As I looked at that dream, I gained insight about our lives here on planet Earth. Half of us will succeed with our hopes and wishes and the other half won't. It's not easy living here with all the guns and those who believe that attack gets you something you would want. It never will. Attack comes from weakness not strength, as do judgements. Judgements are killing forces. You are not to judge. Give it to God.

My next dream takes me inside a high school where I'm in the hall looking at display cases. The cases are full of students' art work. No one is in the hall, as I intently gaze at all the crafts and paintings. This work is quite pleasing to me and I find the students' art work advanced. I'm particularly attracted to a large, white hanging paper sculpture. It's shaped like a bullet with different textures created by the folds in the paper, quite a work of art.

I decide to walk to the art department. As I look through the door, I notice most of the tables are lined up-front, complete with various tools and supplies needed for the different art projects. Class is not in session, so there are only a few students scattered around. I walk in and continue to observe how things are done here and the quality of the work produced. I squeeze between the tables and go to a large open area in the back of the room. Ahead of me is a portable folding screen with more of the students' drawings and paintings. Again, I'm quite impressed with the quality of these art works, especially a lithograph print of a group of people.

The art teacher arrives and comes over to me. I tell him how much I've enjoyed his students' work. He seems to be a very progressive man, intelligent and of strong character, about forty years old. I say to him, "I've been wondering what it's like to be an art teacher. What I don't like about it is that art teachers tend to spend all their time teaching. Teachers don't have much time to work on their own creations. I wouldn't want to give up my own art work for teaching art. You have done this, too. "I can see he doesn't like me pointing out this fact to him, though he doesn't deny it.

I turn and notice a jewelry section in the art room where a young woman teacher is helping two students. She says to me, "I just come in part time to help out with the jewelry department." She shows me a ring she is assisting one of the student to make. This piece is impressive. I think the quality is comparable to a college graduate student, majoring in jewelry. She shows me how it goes on the hand. The ring fits between two fingers and has a bracelet piece that goes across the back of the hand, shaped in one sculptural piece. I examine it closer to see how it was made. It was formed in halves with dyes, then hammered with chasing tools. The halves were soldered together making a hollow form. The ring has a clear almond shape opal stone set with a band around the middle of the stone. The stone is suspended on a silver spike, quite a project!

I take one last sweeping look around the art room. My eyes stop at a crack between the wall and the floor. Through the split I can see the art teacher down in the basement. I wonder what he's doing.

Dreams are a good place to see some great art. Ideas can be brought back with you to use in your life. My statement about being an art teacher has been my position since I was in high school and still hasn't changed. Though, I've had my grandson ask me to show him how to make a ring, which I did. He then lost it playing in our lake. I do use my inner-mind, different from my train of thought, when creating. I can ask it for solutions to painting problems, then wait for the answer as I continue to work. It will come floating in and I will happily recognize it. Perhaps the art teacher in my dream went to the basement to think about his art work.

In my next dream, I'm with a group of people and we are entering a white, wooden church, possible built during the American Revolution. I can't tell what denomination this church is because there are no symbols or signs in the foyer. Everyone files up some stairs to a small landing, where they all sit down, cross-legged on the floor. The floor is so crowded I can't find a place to sit. It's quiet as they concentrate on some inner voice.

I see a hallway that slants upward through the church. I wander through these curved halls, until I arrive at a small door at the topmost center of the building. I feel this is the energy source for the church. I'm surprised when I open the door. Inside is a gold foundry. This church is in the gold business.

I hear an alarm going off, signaling the Church is under attack, and the people inside are going to be killed. I run back down the hall a little way to find a place to hide from the invaders. I know I can find a place where they won't find me. I see a small closet door which I open. It contains a large bell. I squeeze inside shutting the door. Once inside the closet, the thought of being killed becomes unimportant to me. I come out and walk all the way down to the foyer again, where I first entered. There are some people mingling about. I know from a long slot in the opposite wall, the products of this Church will emerge. The new product might be different, for the invaders have put silver into the gold foundry, but the result was still the same.

The slot in the wall opens and a new precious metal rolls out in sheet form about three feet wide. I tell the people standing nearby to catch the sheet metal. I reach out my hands and grab its edges, then I remember it must be tremendously hot from the furnace! We shouldn't touch it, although it doesn't seem to have hurt my hands. I tell the people to take off their clothes and lay them down on the floor to give the metal a clean and protected place to land.

I study the surface of the metal. In the mix of the metals, a design has appeared of numerous, delicate star flowers with gold centers, so beautiful to see. The background has a marble effect created by the mixtures of the metals in their pure form.

When I ponder this dream, I think a white church without denomination means truth will come to all people, regardless of race or creed, through no special religion. Prayer and meditation are important, as the people on the second floor demonstrated. I continued up-ward to the source, to know where we come from the gold of God, the Father. The alarm was my fear about religious persecution. Hiding in the bell closet where my fear disappears, was like a bell to proclaim what I had been given to share with others and the world.

To receive the gold, a product of precious knowledge, one must be naked, free of made up beliefs about themselves and their brothers and sisters. The mixtures of valuable metals represent all religions combined in the glory of God. Thus creating beautiful gold star individuals who will go forth in love and peace. The manifestation of Jesus through THE COURSE IN MIRACLES was like this gold.

I dream of a large, square indoor swimming pool about twenty feet deep. I see four aquatic, ballet swimmers each step up to a corner of the pool. From there, they will simultaneously dive to the bottom of the pool. Once at the bottom, they will cross over each other and ascend to opposite corners. They are to do this all in one breath, quite an amazing feat. I watch them dive to the bottom. I marveling at their breath control. As they ascend, I don't find the young woman diver who had been at the corner closest to me. Something has gone wrong. I quickly dive in the pool to see if I can help. I find her at the bottom of the pool lying motionless. I amazed to discover that I too, can swim this far with just one breath. The woman doesn't appear to have drowned. She just stopped without any apparent will to go father. Dead- in-the-water, so to speak, her breath trapped inside her.

I attempt to pick her up from the bottom by wrapping my arms around her thighs and holding her up-right. However, I find she's too heavy to carry to the top. I have to lay her back down and still I don't feel like I'm running out of air. Then she motions for me to leave her be. She apparently knows what she's doing and prefers to stay underwater for now.

This dream illustrated that sometimes we have to wait till the time is right for us. With no ideas about what to do next, she waits before ascending to the surface and continuing on with her life. Pending divorce can become a major, spiritual road block. I wanted to save myself and move on, but don't push the flow as the dream suggested.

I dream I'm in a college where some of the students have been called into a large room with tables and chairs. They sit down around the tables and wait for instructions. Our teacher has planned that our groups will put on four separate theater productions. The teacher, to keep it fair, has us count off by fours around the room and same numbers will have their own group. As the count off begins, I wonder what number I will have as the students closer to me begin to say their numbers. One student says "zero" and a few others follow suit. This confuses me and I wonder if it is legitimate to say zero?

I feel mixed up about where the count is when it's my turn, I say, "Two." When the count is finished and the students leave with their different groups to work on their production. I go to the office to ask about zeros being used. When I return, everyone has gone to their rooms. I'm not sure which room the twos went to, but then I remember someone in the office told me where the twos were rehearsing. I cross the multipurpose room and open a door on the other side.

As I enter the class room, I note that all the students are seated. They have already picked the topic of their play. Everyone turns and looks at me, then they cheer and clap for me! I guess I'm a talented, creative artist and they're very glad to have me on their team, enhancing their chances to win.

We are to do a parody of a college art department. I wished I'd been there earlier to help pick out the topic. This one doesn't particularly turn me on. I'll have to see what I can do with it since they have already decided. I suggest to the group we have a narrator on stage acting as the art teacher, who is giving the audience an art lessons. The rest of us will dress-up as crayons and paint brushes, with a white back-drop on the stage to represent a piece of paper or canvas. We act out what the art teacher is saying to the audience in our humorous ways. I see this happening in my mind.

I only attended the University of Washington for two years. I was an art major. It was hard, because I had my baby Sasha to nurse, so I setup my classes in between. Ralph would watch her while I was gone. He had a job as a dog and cat license inspector, in which he had a quota each day. It gave him a flexible schedule. I didn't think I needed an art degree to paint, though later I found out most people didn't know what good art was, so they used your credentials to decide. In the dream I was given appreciation for my career choice of being a creative artist. I had to express who I was in my own way. I like to know the rules, as my concern about zero suggested. The challenge was to turn art into money to live on.

I'm watching Leonard, our therapist in the next dream who is talking to two dark haired men. They are showing him how to take a drug which changes ones normal sensation and consciousness. I feel Leonard is leading himself astray. He doesn't need this drug. If he explores himself naturally, he will find the ability to change what needs changing in his life and receive information in a new, exciting way.

Now he's drunk and soggy with the chemical. His consciousness is distorted and blurred, not enhanced. I'm disgusted with his drug trip, but I won't lecture him or give him any advice. We travel to another building. On the way, Leonard questions these men about the sensations he is feeling, as to whether this is what he should be expecting. They reassure him.

While we are at this building, a man is murdered. The authorities are coming to investigate the crime. I know I didn't do it and Leonard will be blamed for the death. I say to Leonard, "You will be accused of the murder, because you are intoxicated with the drug. You can't remember what you did while high on the drug." Innocent pleasure has gone deadly.

I've never been a drug fan; whether psychedelic, pot or mushrooms, though I've tried a little. It only confirmed my dislike of the drug induced state. You give up your natural control over yourself. I've also heard about many bad trips. Look naturally within yourself: dreams, prayer, and mediation are ways to know who you really are and from where you come. You will be rewarded for looking in the right places.

I find myself going to a place where I use to work in my next dream. I'm at Boehm's Candy Kitchen, only the sales counters are in the same room with the cutting and dipping department. I walk by the glass counters full of chocolate candies to a back wall, where there are tables for cutting chews and bins for dipping chocolates. The same kind of chocolate work I used to do is being performed by a young, African American man. It feels good to see my past job, I'd enjoyed. I feel hungry for a piece of dark chocolate, so I sneak a dark chocolate covered caramel. I move toward the center of the store. Here I can nonchalantly eat it, except I sense that man who is doing my job knows I have a piece of candy. I can see the reflection of his face like a mirror in a round chocolate sheet leaning against the wall. I remember, Julius gives me all the candy I would want, so there's no need to sneak a piece. I set the candy aside and go back over to the African American. Next to him is another man cutting caramel chews. A job I use to do well.

Julius, the owner strolls in and comes over to complement the young man about the nice job he's doing cutting the caramels all the same size. Julius doesn't seem to see me, even though I'm standing next to him. Maybe I'm invisible in the dream. Everyone starts munching on whatever piece of candy they're working on. Still, Julius doesn't notice me. I say, "Everyone is having their lunch in candy today." After I say this, Julius turns to some dishes of food sitting on the top of the counter. He's going to eat nutritious food instead.

As I reflect on this dream, I was probably reviewing a job I liked in the past knowing I'd be faced with finding a new job when my marriage ended. I had worked at Boehm's Candy Kitchen when I was pregnant with Sonia, hand dipping chocolates and cutting chews. Then it was all done by women. I loved standing outside the bathroom licking the chocolate off my hands before going in. Two of the young women were best friends, and they didn't like Julius hiring me, as both thought I wasn't needed. I intruded on their private conversations. They were unpleasant to me, but I quit before my second baby was born.

My dream situation worsens. I'm staying in a hotel where I eat something hard, then my back molar breaks. I think, *Well that takes care of that tooth. I'll have to see the dentist for sure to get it fixed.* I reach inside my mouth to feel the tooth and find the tooth has broken into about five pieces. It's no more.

A man walks by and says to me, "Save the pieces of the tooth and the dentist can glue them together to make you a matching false tooth." This sounds impossible to me, to match all those crumbed pieces. I dismiss the whole dentist idea.

Later, I'm chewing some caramel candy, when I discover the caramel is sticking to my bottom teeth, causing them to loosen. I reach into my mouth to carefully try to separate the sticky caramel from my teeth. This doesn't work and I hear some of the roots of my teeth breaking off, though there's no pain. I can feel some very loose molars, too. As I bring the caramel out of my mouth, a couple of my back molars are embedded in it! I notice they're quite large for back molars. My mouth feels full of broken pieces of teeth and silver chunks of fillings. In short, a horror of a problem for a dentist. I finally manage to get my mouth cleaned out. I stand in front of a mirror surveying the damage. I have only one small tooth remaining on the left bottom jaw. I wish my dentist had not pulled one of my upper wisdom teeth, because he didn't want to fill it. At least I'd have one molar to chew on. There're a few bottom teeth missing on the right side. I'd better get to the dentist as soon as possible before the rest of my teeth fall out! I'm not worried about my appearance. I know the dentist can make me a set of false teeth that will look like my own to anyone else. I feel like a baby with bare gums.

I rush to the telephone to call my dentist. I seem to be having trouble finding the right phone number to get the call through. Finally, the receptionist answers. She says the doctor is not there. I decide to skip making an appointment and drop by in person, so he can take care of my mouth right away. I think to myself, *I will just have to grow a new set of teeth.* I believe I can do this, though I've never heard of anyone doing this before.

When I woke up, I was so glad to have all my teeth and they were just fine. At the time, I didn't know what to make of this dream. Now, I think my teeth represented old values that were creating sticky problems for me, when dealing with chewing my life food. Big changes were needed like new teeth. The first broken tooth, a hard situation, I really didn't want to deal with the problem so the dream upped the ante. I'd have to do something serious after losing most of my teeth. Often, we try earth solutions in dreams, thus my search for a dentist. As I processed that dream, I realized my dental problems represented spiritual problems. I thought I could grow a new set of teeth (beliefs). This would take some time in my life after finding THE COURSE IN MIRACLES, lessons in truth, new teeth.

My next dream takes me back in time to take another look at a direction I didn't take. I'm at my parents' house in Pasco. I walk out the front door toward my car, which turns out to be my old high school boyfriend Gene's car. It's a white "53" Studebaker. (Starting when I was a sophomore and Gene was a senior, we dated for two years.) Apparently, in this dream, when I broke-up with him, he gave me his car. Diana, my best girlfriend since seventh grade, is in the front seat with me. She's all dolled up without a hair out of place.

We drive down the street toward the end of the block where Gene's oldest brother's family lives. The Studebaker transforms into a convertible. As we pass their house, I see Gene sitting in the front yard with his brother. Gene looks shocked at the unexpected sight of his old car with Diana and me inside it. (I hadn't seen him in ten years). He glances down at the ground to hide his hurt feelings about my ending the relationship.

Both Gene and I seem unattached and available for a relationship in the dream, though we are both younger than we are now. I feel interested in Gene. I drive across the highway with Diana to Gene's parents' house. They lived quite close to my parent's home. I'm greeted by Gene's mother, who has passed away now in our regular time. Around the side of their house comes Duane, Gene's younger brother. He looks unchanged since I last saw him thirteen years ago. At this point, something of mine rolls out of Gene's car into their backyard. I ask Duane to retrieve it for me, since I'm uncertain of my relationship with these old friends. I don't feel I have the right to go into their backyard. Duane brings me back my lost possession. In the dream it wasn't revealed to me what it was.

As I thought about this dream, I seemed to be having a past, drive-by second look at a relationship I'd left behind. Driving Gene's car, definitely put me in the right time frame. Gene and I spent a lot of time in his "53" Studebaker, so many memories with first love. What was mine that fell out of the car, wasn't my virginity. Maybe, it was the fact that I wasn't going to be joining their family. Gene and I did have a lot in common. We both liked to draw, his mechanical drawing and mine fine art. We were the Capricorn and Pisces connection, earth and water, nurturing, but I found him too conservative and judgmental about some of my behavior, such as when I got tipsy drinking my parent's spiked punch at home.

Gene was tall and willowy and held our high school record in pole vaulting. When he went away to California for Army Reserve training for six months, he didn't want me to date anyone else. I didn't want that arrangement, which eventually led to my breaking up with him. If he hadn't hung on so tightly, I might have been there for him when he returned. I just felt I was too young to be that committed.

I did see him ten years later at my tenth class reunion dinner. We were both married. I knew who he'd married, because I'd worked with her mother doing commercial art for the Safeway stores. Gene came over to our table and pulled up a chair to talk with me. I found this to be a friendly gesture. Ralph was there, too. I noticed Gene had gained about forty pounds and looked like his father. We had barely started a conversation, when Gene's wife came over and grabbed him by the ear, pulling him back to their table. How embarrassing! I couldn't believe anyone would really do that to someone. Although I had heard of it being done to children, never a grown man! Gene's a nice, gentle man, maybe, too much so. I guess he got a dominating wife.

Chapter Twenty-Nine

I dream of a snow field with Ralph starting across the field without me. I'm to stay behind to experience the feelings of being left behind. I don't want to do this. I know I can write my own script, and events don't have to be one way. I can go with him if I like. I happily run after him through the snow. When I catch up with Ralph, he's glad to see me but he firmly says, putting his hands on my shoulders and looking me right in the eyes, "This is not what you're supposed to do. You're to stay behind." I feel like a disappointed child. *This isn't what I want!*

Next, I have five dreams in a row. In them I'm assigned a role in a drama which I refuse to play each time. I have a feeling I have done this before.

On waking, I find myself wondering what I'm avoiding. Perhaps, I'm to play different roles to experience how it feels and see what I do when faced with a new situation. I can't make other people do what they really don't want to do, so I have to take care of myself. If it's being left behind, who likes that? Unless, you don't want to go. Ralph was always threatening to leave me, particularly when things were not going his way. I finally told him to leave, if he really didn't care about me or the family. He stayed that time. Guess it wasn't the end of the problem. What about stamina, to stick it out through good and tough times? But if the values are wrong, it won't work anyway. Let it go. Start over with hopefully some workable rules. Then to make peace, we need to embrace forgiveness.

I've come across another past life dream. In the dream I find myself out in a desert area. Near me is a row of mud houses all connected together? Behind them stands a large stone temple. I'm a slender, brown skinned woman with long black hair. I'm one of a troupe of dancers, maybe a dozen or more, who will be performing by the temple. We have a director who is dark haired with a goatee. He is bare from the waist up and wears a white skirt.

We have just completed a mathematical dance of great significance. Performing the dance creates a powerful energy like a magic spell. We wear hip hugging pants that billow and are made with a dense fabric. Gold coins are sewn close together down each leg. Our costume is completed with a pink vest like a bustier leaving our brown midriffs and long arms bare. The coins jingle and shimmer in the sunlight as we move in a slow rhythmic pattern. We dance in a circle facing each other with flowing intricate steps, forward then backward.

As I dance left of the temple, I see a regiment of people above us in regimented lines. They take turns in formation as they look down upon our natural stage shaped from the terrain. The people go on as far as I can see across the plain waiting for their turn to watch.

Later, I go into a mud hut to change again into my dance outfit. Another shift of women dancers has just finished. They hang their costumes up on pegs so the next group can use them. Apparently, this dance goes on all day. I look for my gold pantaloons. Mine are decorated in gold coins, but some pants don't have coins. At last I find them and dress to join the next troupe of dancers.

As evening descends and gets darker, the dancing is over. Now I'm inside the King's stone temple behind our huts. A young, handsome General comes over to me and asks, "Where's the King?" I know he wants to assassinate him, and take control of the country. I don't seem to have any moral feelings about whether the King is killed or not. I'm aware the King is a weak and scared person.

I say to the General, "Beware for the King. He has a fast gun." The General draws his long dagger, because the King is in the next room hiding with another man. The General's knife flies around the corner and the fight begins. I'm afraid and flee.

I'm standing outside on one of the temple's balconies looking into the night. I stare at our dance director who is on a high overhanging rock. His body is aglow with light as he prays. I think *what a dramatic effect. This will really amaze the people.*

The dream is a slice of a past life. Apparently, there was a man of great knowledge back then, too working his feats of miracles. I worked directly with him as one of his dancers. I think the energy was used to move heavy objects.

To continue about the realm of self-knowledge, I dream of seeing a large unfinished, silver colored ring band. This ring is being shown to me by another who I can't see, but I hear his voice and feel his presence close at hand. The ring symbolizes our spiritual unity, an integration of body and soul. I've been working on this theme. I become very excited, because I know how to finish the ring. I will achieve this for myself in this lifetime. A Voice says, "You're to help others in their spiritual growth. You're to finish the ring slowly, not quickly."

Scene changes, I see Reverend A, the minster of the church I attended with my parents while I was growing up. He stands in the interior of a church. He doesn't speak and is portraying patience and steadiness.

The Voice says, "And if the ring is dropped?"

I finish by saying, "Then I will slip backward." I'm cheerful because I understand the lesson and my part.

I awake happy. I'm on the right path in life and the next dream shows me about this. I'm standing on a pier that stretches out into an ocean inlet. Across from me and this body of water is a jetty with a warehouse. The breeze from the ocean is misty and the environment feels strangely wild and alive. I have a salmon pole in my hands. I cast my line to my right and down currant. Someone else is on the dock with me, a man, though his presence is in the background. I follow my line with my eyes across the surface of the active waves. Then zing, I have a strike! I wait and don't reel immediately, because I want to be sure the fish has taken the bait. There's a second hit

DREAMING INSIDE OUT

on my line. Now I reel the tugging, fighting fish in. When I get a glimpse of the size of my salmon, I'm proud. It's the largest fish I've ever caught! I lift the salmon out of the water and onto the dock with my pole. On closer look, I'm astonished to find that I have two fish, not one. Obviously, my first strike was a large beautiful salmon, but then a second and larger salmon swallowed the first fish. I can see both fish now because the second fish's head is cut away and reveals the first salmon. This second salmon puzzles me. At the head, worn away flesh reveals pink-red meat. This salmon has had a rough spawning journey. He's must be glad to finally be caught with this perfect salmon inside.

As I think about this dream, maybe I'm the second beat-up salmon looking for a better life. Now I've caught and swallowed my spiritual inner-fish. I've given up my head to let my first salmon guild me home to the Father. It's time to give thanks. Dreams can show you amazing grace.

My troubles are not over, as I find myself in a room in my next dream. In one corner of this room two bar stools sit. On the first stool a beautiful peacock perches with his tail fully spread. On the other stool rests a shoe. I walk toward the stools sitting side by side. As I approach the peacock slowly falls backward and breaks his tail against the wall. I'm agitated because I feel, maybe I'm to blame for the peacock's fall. The peacock pulls himself together and gingerly slinks away without a tail.

I reach down and pick up the mass of tail feathers still clinging together like a partly spread fan. While I'm holding the fan, it slowly turns into a sleeping hen. She awakens and flutters out of my hands. The hen leaves in the direction the peacock. I notice there are still some of the peacock's colorful feathers, singularly scattered on the floor. I stoop and collect the bright feathers, thinking that something artistic could be made from them. As I hold the feathers, they turn into a small dog that bites me. The dog turns into a black cat which also bites me! I'm extremely upset and startled. I need to get this situation under control!

I grab the cat's head and with both of my hands stretching its jaws open, so it can't bite me. I'm surprise at the amount of energy

I expend to do this. The struggling cat changes into a set of jaws of human teeth which I continue to force open so I'm not bitten again. I need a solution to this problem. Then the teeth become two small, white metal boxes, about the size of an aspirin tablet can. I know I have to keep the two boxes together, so holding them side by side, I put them in my mouth and bite down with all my strength. It's an extremely powerful clamp. *I think I probably bit with my real teeth in my sleep.* On removing the boxes, I see my crushing teeth marks left that welded the two boxes together. I feel good about this result and a sense of accomplishment! I vaguely remember an older woman assisting me with the boxes' solution.

So, what's this all about? For me, a peacock represents strutting, beautiful vanity. Losing his tail, he now has nothing to strut about. I've given up some vanity. Picking up the tail, awakens the sleeping hen, myself. Trying to save the feathers for more self-enhancing decoration will bite me, dog and cat, domestic life. Having no vanity will stop the biting, eventually showing human teeth, back to the self. Two white metal boxes, the self I think I am, needs to come together with my spiritual self, body and soul alignment. I need to keep them together. "I am not a body. I am free for I am still as God created me," from THE COURSE IN MIRACLES book.

Ralph and I took several more self-growth seminars. In one seminar John Enright had a theory about making changes you wanted in your life. First you have to get in contact with the space right below where you wanted to be, and really feel what it's like for you. Then you could move up into the new thought area and make it yours.

Being a highly visual person, I dream of seeing two white lines floating in the air in front of me. These lines represent John Enright's theory. I walk up to the lower line which is about chest level to me. I let in the experience that's there for me. All of a sudden, a strong laser beam hits the pit of my stomach followed by an immediate realization of what I'm about. I propel upward to the higher line. Here, I feel joy and complete comfort. I step back from the two lines and circle around them from a distance. I puzzle this theory trying to remember the first realization I experienced on the lower level. It's in me somewhere.

Here's another dream along the same theme. I dream someone places a leaf into my hand. Then a voice says to me, "Tell me how the leaf is different than it was before?"

I carefully inspect the leaf by holding it up to the sky so I can see the veins and inner structure better. Then I see it! The vein pattern of the leaf has changed and it swirls up from the stem in a soft wave like pattern, instead of the straight center stem with veins off of it. I feel excited and happy. I quickly bend down and pick up a piece of wood from the ground. Again, I notice the change in the grain of the wood from concentric to wavy.

My life must be flowing more smoothly, or I should go in a calmer, gentler manner. That would evolve not letting upsetting events bother me. It's just crazy life.

So I've experienced some spiritual progress as is reflected in my inner-life, but I still have so much to learn every day. Troubles with my marriage are far from over as my next dream shows.

I am sleeping next to Ralph, when I dream that some older, substantial trees on the back of our property have fallen down. Still dreaming, I waken and go to our front door. From here I peer up our driveway toward the river. There is an ominous looking large pool of water on the road out front and on our driveway. I think, *Oh, no. The river must have flooded late last night!* I quickly call Ralph to alert him to our problem. We didn't even know the river had flooded. But now, I recall the fallen trees on our back lot. I say, "I remember about having a realization something was happening as we slept. The soil must have been so wet that the roots had nothing firm to cling to and four large trees fell in the back area."

Ralph says, "Quick, check the tree nursery and see what damages we have received."

I look out our bedroom window, as Ralph goes outside to inspect. I see the tree farm has heavy damages. A lot of newly planted, small trees have been completely bent over or washed away. (More damage than our first real flood of Snoqualmie River.)

I walk across our front property to the river bank to check out what happened. I'm shocked and amazed as I gaze down onto the riverbed. An avalanche of water must have rushed through causing a flash flood! The riverbed is now a deep gorge littered with logs from Weyerhaeuser's operation upstream. A small flow of water trickles at the bottom of the gorge carved out by the rushing water. I'm incredibly impress by the power of the water to do all this! Our house and tree farm are lucky to be still standing.

This same night before I had my last dream, I also dreamed I had awakened to find Ralph is not in our bed. Then I heard him in the bathroom at the end of our kitchen. I feel Ralph is very angry with me. As he walks through the dark kitchen toward our bed, I imagine that he is concealing a butcher knife in his hand and intends to murder me! With that thought, I become extremely afraid. I wonder if I should jump up and escape before he has the chance to kill me. I decide to take the risk. If he's going to kill me, he will, so why fight it. I'll die that way. I feel relief as Ralph crawls into bed beside me without any knife.

Pondering the dream, I wondered to myself, *Did I really perceive people wanted to kill me when I didn't do what they wanted me to do?* I deliberately scared myself. Luckily, I didn't jump out of bed and scare Ralph, too. The dream was showing the power of anger when it's not dealt with, what destruction it can cause.

This next dream takes me through imagined fear and how it escalates. In my dream, I'm in a rather rundown residential part of Spokane. I'm walking down the street when suddenly, I have a paranoid thought. I'm alone in an unfamiliar area of town where I shouldn't be walking for safety reasons. This is how some women get mugged or raped. I hurriedly glance over my shoulder to see if any men are lurking around. I'm shocked to see all the front doors opening on the block with a man appearing on each door step. They are waiting for me to pass them! I've got to get out of here fast!

I rush across the street and head in the opposite direction. I notice a white, wooden framed house that looks like it might be a safe haven for me to take shelter. I can hear all the men grumbling together to decide what to do about me. I sneak a look back and see one of the men's Doberman Pinscher is running after me. I hurry to the front steps of the white house. A large, red Irish Setter stands at the top of the steps and greets me warmly. The Doberman is now right behind me. I dodge behind the Irish setter who doesn't like the presence of the Doberman. The Setter starts to growl at the Doberman. I open the front door and burst into the living room. On the couch sits an old, white haired woman who smiles a welcome to me. I know it will be alright to hide in this house. I walk into the kitchen and look around. Off the kitchen is a small laundry room. From here, I can detect the ring leader of the men chasing after me, enter the front room of the white house searching for me. I must hide quickly! I scramble under a pile of dirty, white clothes lying on the floor by the washing machine ready to be washed.

I hear his footsteps walking through the kitchen toward the laundry room, where he stops. He apparently doesn't see me under the dirty clothes and retreats back through the house, leaving. Maybe he doesn't like this white house? I don't really feel safe in the white house anymore because anyone can enter as easily as I did. No one is denied access. I decide to sneak out of the house when I think everyone has given up and gone home.

Later, I peek out the front door. It looks clear, so I hurry out the door to the street curb, where I find an old Model T-Ford parked. I jump in and drive off. There is another woman in the front seat with me, perhaps she was waiting for me. As soon as the car moves away from the curb, all the men come running out of their houses and start chasing after us. We race all through the town. We just manage to stay ahead of the pursuers. Finally, the police intercept us and arrest all of us. I'm bemused and relieved to finally have the chase over.

We are all loaded-up and taken to prison, which turns out to be an old abandon factory overlooking a waterway. Men and women are all locked-up together on the second floor. The men go off together to play poker and the women go to the bunk room to gossip.

I didn't resolve this dream and law and order stepped in to stop the craziness. We were imprisoned until I was ready to deal with this fear that had been instilled and passed around a lot in my past. The white house was the dwelling place of my higher self, the only place where I'm going to find resolution along with truth and peace. No right choices are made outside of the white house, only more egomania was shown. I needed to calm down, get out from under my dirty clothes (fear thoughts) and go sit down with the white haired lady on the couch and have a heart to heart talk.

I will say, "If you have to go somewhere by yourself, don't look for trouble, bless the men, surround yourself with white light and don't loiter. You are safe in God's loving care."

I found a poem I wrote in 1976 describing my troubles with self.

The Center of Me

When pain wracks my stomach and brain,
It's so hard to say that hurts me so!
I'd rather say,
I don't like what you're doing and
give you my thoughts on the issues brewing.
I hid my pain far below
like a love I'm afraid to grow.
I don't want you to know
I love with all my heart and soul.
You can hurt me more than anyone I know.
Hiding doesn't change the truth,
nor will pain wipe away love's gains.
To love is to open myself
to the spectrum of joy and hurt.
The jewels are found along with rock and dirt.
Protecting my feelings only prolongs my pain.
Not experiencing my love is like water down the drain.
Not trusting my feelings, kills my ability to act,
keeps me in doubt from finding out what I'm about.
I won't live my life measuring and returning
exactly what others put out.
It doesn't matter and keeps me controlled by the game.
I don't have to wait and see what he will do.

I know what's right for me and the quality I choose.
That's something I will not lose.
I'll keep putting out what I know I can use.
I won't change any of my love and caring, touch and sharing.
I will keep faith with myself and all that I am.

As I examined my box of dream notebooks, it was obvious that there are probably enough dreams for a few more books! Thirteen years of dream writing covers a lot of time to unfold my story. Those of you who have made it to the end of my first book DREAMING INSIDE OUT, I thank you. I hope you've learned how we live our lives from the inside out. I'm now thirty years old in the dream notebooks, so a couple of years have gone by.

Write your dreams down and be guided by your inner soul to become aware of what's ahead and the inner-working of your true God's self.

THE END

www.ingramcontent.com/pod-product-compliance
Lightning Source LLC
Chambersburg PA
CBHW050554300426
44112CB00013B/1907